Modern Peacemakers

Nelson Mandela

Ending Apartheid in South Africa

MODERN PEACEMAKERS

Modern Peacemakers

Nelson Mandela

Ending Apartheid in South Africa

Samuel Willard Crompton

CHELSEA HOUSE
PUBLISHERS
An imprint of Infobase Publishing

Nelson Mandela

Copyright © 2007 by Infobase Publishing

Chelsea House
An imprint of Infobase Publishing
132 West 31st Street
New York NY 10001

Library of Congress Cataloging-in-Publication Data
Crompton, Samuel Willard.
  Nelson Mandela : ending apartheid in South Africa / Samuel Willard Crompton.
    p. cm. — (Modern peacemakers)
  Includes bibliographical references and index.
  Audience: Grades 9-12.
  ISBN 0-7910-8997-5 (hardcover)
    1. Mandela, Nelson, 1918–   —Juvenile literature. 2. Presidents—South Africa—Biography—Juvenile literature. 3. Anti-apartheid activists—South Africa—Biography—Juvenile literature. 4. Apartheid—South Africa—History—20th century—Juvenile literature. 5. South Africa—Politics and government—1948–1994—Juvenile literature. 6. South Africa —Politics and government—1994– —Juvenile literature. 7. South Africa—Race relations—History—20th century—Juvenile literature. I. Title.
  DT1974.C76 2006
  968.06'5092—dc22
  [B]   2006017555

Text design by Annie O'Donnell
Cover design by Takeshi Takahashi

Printed in the United States of America

Bang FOF 10 9 8 7 6 5 4 3 2 1

This book is printed on acid-free paper.

TABLE OF CONTENTS

CHAPTER 1

Six Thousand Miles Apart

Nelson Mandela and Martin Luther King Jr. never met. Separated by a great ocean and 6,000 miles, they carried on their struggles for freedom on parallel tracks but never had the opportunity to share what they learned with one another.

Born in 1918, Nelson Mandela was 11 years older than his American counterpart, but in the spring of 1964, one could say that Martin Luther King Jr. had achieved more. Mandela was about to be sentenced for a series of crimes, and King was about to taste some of the hard-won fruits of the past few years. Again, one wonders what the two men could have done if they had been able to work together. As it was, several major events took place in June 1964 that affected both of their causes.

CIVIL RIGHTS IN THE UNITED STATES

Born in 1929, Martin Luther King Jr. was 35 in the spring of 1964. The son of a prominent minister, King had followed in his father's footsteps. During the late 1950s, he led a number of protests for civil rights in the United States. King's actions won him the admiration of many, but the hatred of many others. His crowning moment came in August 1963, when he addressed an enormous crowd at the National Mall during a massive march on Washington, D.C. In one of the most inspired speeches of an inspired lifetime, King told his listeners that he had a dream of a color-blind society: a society in which people would be judged by their character rather than by the color of their skin. Justly hailed as one of the great speeches of American history, indeed in the history of the world, the "I Have a Dream" speech became Dr. King's signature moment. The struggle continued, however.

In the spring of 1964, Martin Luther King Jr. was in St. Augustine, Florida. He went there because the residents of this southern city were some of the most vehement defenders of segregation in the United States. The oldest city in the country, St. Augustine had been founded by Spanish settlers in 1565 and was about to celebrate its 400th anniversary. Well aware of this, King had traveled to St. Augustine, hoping to demonstrate the strength of the civil rights movement.

If King could convince the people of St. Augustine to desegregate, it would be a great accomplishment. Perhaps he wanted his hoped-for success to coincide with a major legislative event, for a logjam had finally broken in the U. S. Congress. The Civil Rights Act of 1964 appeared ready to win approval.

In the aftermath of King's "I Have a Dream" speech, many congressmen and senators had been persuaded to back the cause of civil rights. The Civil Rights Act of 1964, containing many clauses regarding voting and voting rights, had passed the U.S. House of Representatives in February 1964, but it was stalled in the U.S. Senate. A majority of senators favored the bill, but a small minority who opposed the act had the power to block it through use of a filibuster.

The act of filibustering developed in the nineteenth century. A minority of U.S. senators could prevent a yes-or-no vote from taking place by speaking endlessly, or just by threatening to speak endlessly. For 75 days, in the spring of 1964, a small minority of senators blocked an up-or-down vote on the Civil Rights Act. The resistance finally cracked, however, on June 10.

Senator Everett Dirksen of Illinois was a Republican in favor of many aspects of the civil rights movement. He worked his way around the Senate floor, and when the votes were called in the afternoon on June 10, the Senate voted 72 to 29 in favor of an up-or-down vote. A two-thirds majority of 67 votes was required to break the deadlock, and Dirksen had succeeded. President Lyndon B. Johnson indicated he would sign the Civil Rights Act; that ceremony would take place on July 2, 1964.

Millions of Americans, black and white, rejoiced; millions of others, mostly white, though, were angered by the passage of the bill. The great step had been taken, however. There were major celebrations, in Washington, D.C., especially, but the greatest leader of the movement was not on hand to rejoice with his followers. Martin Luther King Jr. was still in St. Augustine.

King had run into great resistance, stronger even than he had feared. The white majority in the city was resolutely opposed to desegregation, and the city government supported the people. There were scuffles, people on both sides were injured, and the situation had the potential to become very ugly. Feeling desperate, Martin Luther King Jr. allowed himself to be arrested. He and 17 comrades were arrested outside the Monson Hotel restaurant, whose owner had refused to serve African Americans.

King spent that night in solitary confinement. Later he admitted this was one of his lowest moments, and that the St. Augustine jail was one of the worst he had encountered. King knew a great deal about jails; he had written his remarkable "Letter from Birmingham Jail" while in prison in Birmingham, Alabama, just a year earlier.

King was released on bail on June 15, after serving just two nights in the St. Augustine jail. He vowed to continue the struggle, but he knew it would have to be in another time and place. The resistance in St. Augustine was, for the moment, too strong, too determined. In fact, it was one of the bastions of defiant Southern segregation.

History of the Nobel Peace Prize

Alfred Nobel died on December 10, 1896. His will, written one year earlier, directed that the vast majority of his fortune—estimated at $9 million—was to be used for the establishment and award of annual prizes in five categories: literature, medicine or physiology, chemistry, physics, and for the "person who had made the greatest contribution to the cause of promoting friendship among nations, disarmament or limitation of armaments, as well as to the establishment and popularization of the Congresses of Peace."*

Ever since, people have marveled at the incongruity between the man, his career, and the award that was named for him. Alfred Nobel was a Swede who spent many years living in other nations; he spent a lot of time in Paris; and he died in Italy. He made his fortune in his thirties by perfecting the manufacture of explosives, which he patented in 1867. This was the beginning of dynamite. How strange that such a man would leave most of his vast fortune to the establishment of international prizes, and that one of them would be the Peace Prize.

The first peace prizes were awarded in 1901. Nobel had established the selection process, by which a committee of five persons chosen by the Norwegian Parliament made the choices. They began a custom of announcing the prizes in October and giving the actual awards on December 10 of each year, the day of Nobel's death.

More than 100 persons and organizations total have been awarded the Nobel Peace Prize. Nobel's will provided that the award could be given to as many as three persons in one year; there have been numerous occasions on which it was given to two persons, and one occasion when it went to three. Examination of the recipient list indicates that the Nobel Prize committees have indeed fulfilled Nobel's intention that the prize should not be limited to one nationalist or ethnic group. But further perusal also shows

So, June 1964 was a time of mixed prospects for the civil rights movement. A great legislative victory had been won, but the people of St. Augustine had proven that legislation cannot

that there have not been many women selected for the honor. Baroness Bertha von Suttner was the first to win, in 1905, but as of 2005, only 10 other female peacemakers have been recognized with the award.

Americans have fared well in the Nobel Peace Prize selection process. President Theodore Roosevelt won the award for mediating the peace conference that ended the Russo-Japanese War; President Woodrow Wilson won it for his work at the peace conference that ended World War I. But there have been some controversial selections, including that of Dr. Henry Kissinger, who, as secretary of state, worked toward ending the U.S. presence in South Vietnam. Kissinger's critics claimed it was a farce for this man, who had been behind so much of U.S. policy that led to the Vietnam War, to receive the Peace Prize.

Two of the biggest events surrounding the Nobel Peace Prize had to do with Middle Eastern diplomacy. In 1979, Israeli Prime Minister Menachem Begin and Egyptian President Anwar Sadat shared the prize for their work on the Camp David Accords that led to peace between their two nations. In 1993, Yitzhak Rabin and Shimon Peres, both of Israel, shared the Nobel Peace Prize with Yasir Arafat; the three men had worked long and hard on the Oslo Accords, which promised peace between Israel and the Palestinian Authority. Sadly, this set of accords did not deliver on its promise.

Alfred Nobel started the process in 1896, and it has been continued by presidents, prime ministers, social workers, medical doctors, and others. Would Nobel have been satisfied? This is difficult to say, but, as some critics even acknowledge, it is better to light one candle than to curse the darkness.

---

*Irwin Adams, *The Nobel Prize*. Boston: G.K. Hall, & Co, 1988, p. 193.

cure all ills, and that people will believe what they will, regardless of what the law says. By an interesting coincidence, Martin Luther King Jr. went into jail on almost the same day as did his great contemporary, Nelson Mandela.

HUMAN RIGHTS IN SOUTH AFRICA

African Americans had a tough fight ahead, but things were even worse for black South Africans. They were the majority of the country's population, but they could not vote, could not run businesses, and had to carry passes whenever they ventured out of their local areas. If the United States was embroiled in a struggle for black civil rights, South Africa was struggling with the question of whether blacks even deserved human rights.

The great evils of segregation and *apartheid* (which means "apartness") were similar, but they had evolved in different ways. Segregation in the United States had developed under a series of laws passed in the 1880s and 1890s, often called the Jim Crow laws. These laws were named after a black character in popular minstrel shows of the time. Apartheid was a more recent concept, born in the 1940s. The white minority population in South Africa stood behind the government in bringing about a complete separation between whites and blacks, Indians (from India), and coloreds (those of mixed race). Unlike the United States, South Africa never claimed they had created institutions that were "separate but equal"—they were simply separate.

Nelson Mandela had become the foremost leader of the resistance movement to apartheid. Born in 1918, he lived a country boyhood before moving to Johannesburg in 1941. He rose to become a prominent attorney—one of the few black lawyers in his country—and joined the great struggle for freedom. By yet another coincidence, Mandela was a leader of the African National Congress (ANC), which had been founded in 1912, just two years after the establishment of the National Association for the Advancement of Colored People (NAACP) in the United States in 1910.

Just as Martin Luther King Jr. had attempted to desegregate St. Augustine on its 400th anniversary, Nelson Mandela and others had started their movement in 1952, the 300th anniversary of the arrival of Dutch settlers in South Africa. For the first few years of the movement, Mandela and others had adhered to a strict policy of nonviolence, but they found their efforts crushed by an ever-increasing use of military and police force by the government. In about 1960, Nelson Mandela made a fateful move toward limited use of violence. He and his fellow resistance fighters continued to reject violence against human beings, but they believed in wrecking or bombing certain government building projects in order to bring attention to their movement for freedom.

Mandela went underground in 1961. Traveling to other African nations, he learned methods of guerrilla fighting. Inspired by the recent success of Fidel Castro in Cuba, Mandela saw himself as a freedom fighter with a gun and hand grenade, a major change for the sophisticated Johannesburg lawyer. South African newspapers dubbed him the "Black Pimpernel," an allusion to the Scarlet Pimpernel who rescued people from the guillotine during the French Revolution.

Perhaps it was fortunate for Nelson Mandela that he was captured in South Africa in 1962. Today we might know him only as a failed guerrilla leader, instead of an example of ultimate victory and forgiveness. In any case, he was arrested and brought to trial with a number of other African National Congress members.

The trial took a long time; 186 witnesses were called and hundreds of thousands of pages of evidence were presented. Most people, however, felt the verdict would be "guilty." Papers in Mandela's handwriting confirmed he had agreed to use violence against political installations, although not against people.

Justice Quartus de Wet handed down his verdict and sentence on June 11, 1964. This was one day after the U.S. Senate had broken the logjam concerning the Civil Rights Act, and one day before Martin Luther King Jr. was arrested in St. Augustine, Florida.

Shown at age 42 in this 1961 photo, Nelson Mandela was known as a "clotheshorse" throughout his life. Whether he dressed in Western-style business suits or in the traditional dress of an African chief, Mandela was almost always handsome and photogenic—qualities that helped him rise in the world.

American readers had their first view of Nelson Mandela in *Time* magazine that month. A tall, handsome man, dressed in a V-neck sweater, Mandela was seated, with his right hand open in a gesture that suggested his ability to persuade. Mandela was also quoted as saying before being sentenced:

> This is the struggle of the African people, inspired by their own suffering and experience. It is a struggle for the right to live. I have cherished the ideal of a democratic and free society, in which all persons live together in harmony and with equal opportunity. It is an ideal which I hope to live for and achieve. But, if need be, my Lord, it is an ideal for which I am prepared to die.[1]

Judge de Wet had the power to condemn these men to death. Sabotage against the state was a major crime. De Wet did not wish to make these men into martyrs, however. He announced that they—Mandela and eight others—were sentenced to lifetime imprisonment. The *Time* magazine article went on:

> Now he will have to live for it in jail. After the sentencing, a crowd held in check by police dogs and armed cops gathered outside the Palace of Justice to watch the prisoners led away. Two Black Marias [secure police vans] purred through the square, then accelerated swiftly through the Pretoria Central Jail. From there the black and "colored" prisoners would be ferried to Robben Island, a former leper colony off the Cape of Good Hope, while the white man would stay in a white prison. As the trucks pulled away, white, black, and brown arms flashed briefly behind the bars in the clench-fisted salute of the African National Congress. From the crowd came a ragged cry: *Amandla nga Weto* [Strength is ours].[2]

Americans would not see another photograph of Mandela again for 27 years.

Even great leaders like Martin Luther King Jr. and Nelson Mandela cannot predict the future. They can guess, surmise, and suppose, but the future holds its surprises for all of us. One of the great ironies of the civil rights movement is that Martin Luther King Jr., a man committed to nonviolence, would die from an assassin's bullet. One of the great points of interest in the story of the African National Congress is that Nelson Mandela, a leader who briefly flirted with the idea of violent revolution, would become one of the most prominent nonviolent leaders of all time.

CHAPTER 2

Tribal Boyhood

N elson Rolihlahla Mandela was born on July 18, 1918. This was the year the Great War, what we now call World War I, ended in Europe. Of course, the baby Mandela knew nothing about the Great War, and his tribal parents and relatives knew only a bit more, but events such as that war would ultimately have an effect on his life and destiny.

Nelson Mandela's autobiography begins with these words:

Apart from life, a strong constitution, and an abiding connection to the Thembu royal house, the only thing my father bestowed upon me at birth was a name, Rolihlahla. In Xhosa, *Rolihlahla* literally means "pulling the branches of a tree," but its colloquial meaning more accurately would be "troublemaker." I do not believe that names are destiny or that my father somehow divined my future, but in later years, friends and relatives would ascribe to my birth name the many storms I have both caused and weathered.[3]

Mandela was also born in the ninety-ninth anniversary year of one of his ancestor's defeats. He was descended from Thembu kings, men who had ruled the Thembu part of the Xhosa tribes for a long time. One of his distant ancestors was defeated by the British in 1819, something young Mandela would remember throughout life. He came from a proud, warlike people who had resisted the Dutch, British, and others for centuries.

THE HISTORY OF SOUTH AFRICA

South Africa is one of the most beautiful lands in the world. It is about 471,000 square miles, making it equal in size to Texas, California, Massachusetts, and Vermont, combined. The country is far enough south of the Equator that it has a climate not unlike that of Europe, which was one of the reasons why the Dutch, British, and others chose to settle there. South Africa is a land of vivid contrasts. The stormy Atlantic Ocean, on its western side, contrasts with the warm, nearly tropical breezes on the Indian Ocean to the east. To those who live along the coast, South Africa can seem like a paradise, but to those condemned to labor in the heat and dust inland, it can seem like hell. South Africa stretches about 900 miles from southwest to northeast and is about 1000 miles across at its widest point. This makes South Africa one of the great nations of the world in terms of physical size and geographic contrast.

Mandela was from the Thembu part of the larger Xhosa tribes, which had been in South Africa since time immemorial. There is no firm agreement about when the Xhosa migrated from more northern parts of the continent to South Africa, but they had plenty of time to develop their culture before white people first arrived.

The Portuguese came first, in the time of Christopher Columbus and Ferdinand Magellan. The Portuguese did nothing more than build a fort or two and name the southern extremity of the continent the Cape of Good Hope. The Dutch, who first came in 1652, however, were quite different: They came to stay.

Holland is a small country, but in the seventeenth century its people migrated to many parts of the world. Some went to New Amsterdam—present-day New York City. Others landed and stayed in parts of the Caribbean; others went as far off as Indonesia. In 1652, a small group went to what they called Cape Town. Their descendants were called Boers, meaning "farmers" or "countrymen," and in the twentieth century, the name was changed to *Afrikaner*. (For the sake of consistency, we will use "Afrikaner" throughout.)

The Afrikaners fought the Xhosa tribes from the beginning. At first these were small conflicts because the Afrikaners were relegated to a small area of South Africa, on its southwestern side. The Napoleonic Wars (1796–1815) changed that, however. Holland was taken over by Napoleon I and the French in about 1795. The British, who were at war with Napoleon, announced that all Dutch colonies worldwide were fair game. The British conquered the Cape Colony, taking it from the Dutch. When the Napoleonic Wars ended in 1815, 103 years before Nelson Mandela's birth, the British took possession of South Africa.

The Xhosa tribes now had to fight two different groups of Europeans: Dutch and British. Both the Dutch and the British had modern weapons, such as the musket and then the rifle. The Africans fought back with spears, speed, and cunning, but they could not stop the inexorable expansion of the European peoples. The British moved east toward the lands where Nelson Mandela was born, and the Dutch moved north-by-northeast to the area where Johannesburg and Pretoria are today.

If the Napoleonic Wars changed the balance of power in Europe and South Africa, the discovery of gold and diamonds did the same. Small finds had been made at Kimberley in the 1860s, but large quantities were found at Johannesburg in 1886. Speculators found gold in layers both above and below ground. Unlike earlier finds in California and elsewhere, the South African gold seemed nearly inexhaustible. The layered structure of the gold meant miners spent years hacking away at gold that was lying in plain sight.

Afrikaner speculators and miners found the gold, and they seemed destined to profit, but the British wanted some of the riches. Under Queen Victoria, Great Britain was the greatest naval and economic power in the world. In 1896, the British tried but failed to stir up a revolution in the Afrikaner section of South Africa. Failing in this, the British started an actual war, called the Anglo-Boer War of 1899 to 1903. The British eventually prevailed, but they created lasting enmity and bitterness between themselves and the Afrikaners. Just a few years after the war ended, the British recognized the hopelessness of governing the entire land by themselves. They created the Union of South Africa in 1910. The new nation was part of the British Commonwealth, but the British and Afrikaners shared political power: The languages of both groups were taught in many schools.

No provision was made in this new government, however, for the black tribal peoples of South Africa, who were the majority in every census. Most black South Africans lacked the education and political knowledge to oppose the white groups, so a small group of middle-class blacks formed the African National Congress (ANC) in 1912, in order to remedy to the lack of any form of self-government for the black people of South Africa. Over time, the ANC became as important to the South African freedom struggle as the NAACP was in the struggle for black civil rights in the United States.

Just two years later, World War I began in Europe. Most British settlers naturally wanted to enter the war on the side of the British, but many Afrikaners resisted being dragged into a "British" war. Although the British view prevailed, many Afrikaners either abstained from the war or carried out resistance movements against the government. Nelson Mandela, who knew his South African history better than many Afrikaner leaders, would often point out the discrepancy to his prison guards; they had struggled

Mandela grew up in a nurturing tribal environment in which there existed no named distinctions among family members; to Mandela, everyone was "brother" or "sister." His father had four wives who most likely lived like these African women, pictured here along a road of the Transkei, transporting goods by head.

for freedom against the British, but they now denied it to blacks. This was the world into which Nelson Mandela was born.

QUNU—MANDELA'S HOME DISTRICT

Mandela's home district was Qunu, in the Transkei section of South Africa. Located between the Drakensburg Mountains to the north and the Indian Ocean to the south, the Transkei is a lovely section of a beautiful country, but it is also very poor.

Mandela's father was Hendry Mandela, and his mother was Fanny Nosekeni. Methodist missionaries had converted his mother to Christianity, and young Mandela was raised in that faith. His father was the grandson of the last of the major Thembu kings, but this does not mean Mandela was ever in line for a throne. Thembu kings had several wives, and Mandela was descended from what was called the "Left Hand" section of the dynasty. He would never become a king, but it was hoped he might become a leading tribal counselor, like his father.

An incident that happened about the time of Mandela's birth had a strong impact on his youth. As a tribal counselor, Mandela's father was a man of some importance in the neighborhood. Hendry Mandela made the mistake of defying a British official over a matter having to do with a black man's herd of cows. Because he resisted, the British magistrate deprived him of his position as tribal counselor. Subsequently, the Mandela family lost about half of their possessions, including cattle, which were seen as the substance of any family's wealth.

Nonetheless, Mandela was a happy youngster. Growing up in the warm, tribal environment of Qunu, he was either related to everyone or felt he was. African tribal groups did not make sharp distinctions like cousin, brother, half-sister, or second cousin. Growing up, Mandela called almost every other child he knew "brother" or "sister." He was also fortunate in having four "mothers." His father had four wives. Mandela had his birth mother and three affectionate stepmothers.

Mandela grew up an athletic, ambitious boy. He delighted in all sorts of games and play, and he once felt his highest ambition was to be the champion stick fighter of his tribe. He never attained this goal but was instead steered in other directions. When he was seven, young Nelson went to school. No other member of his immediate family had done so, but his father rightly decided that some knowledge of the British and their way of learning was necessary, so he sent his young son to a local English school. This is where he acquired the name Nelson, given to him by a teacher who did not wish to have to remember all the children's tribal names.

Mandela was a sober, serious student, but not an outstanding one. He became interested in the British concepts of fair play and equality before the law, and perhaps even as a boy he began to question why they were not applied in all cases. Why did tribal Africans have fewer rights than the British or Afrikaners?

Two years into his schooling, when he was nine, Mandela's world changed abruptly. His father died. The cause was most likely lung disease, but Mandela's father was not diagnosed. In fact, not once in his life had he seen a doctor. This was normal for tribal Africans of the time. Mandela later talked about the event and how it affected him:

> I do not remember experiencing great grief so much as feeling cut adrift. Although my mother was the center of my existence, I defined myself through my father. My father's passing changed my whole life in a way that I did not suspect at the time. After a brief period of mourning, my mother informed me that I would be leaving Qunu. I did not ask her why, or where I was going.[4]

THE GREAT PLACE

Mandela and his mother walked for many hours until they reached a village. Much larger than Qunu, this was Mqhekezweni, or the Great Place. This was the home of Jongintaba, Regent of the Thembu tribe.

Shortly before his death, Hendry Mandela had asked Jongintaba to take on the role of father to young Nelson. Jongintaba made good on his word, and he would now raise Nelson as his own son, in the Great Place. Nelson soon parted from his mother, who, until that time, had been the center of his world. "Her tender look was all the affection and support I needed," Mandela said later, "And as she departed, she turned to me and said, '*Uqinisufokotho Kwedini*' ('Brace yourself, my boy')."[5] She headed off to return to Qunu. Mandela would see very little of her for the next decade.

Luckily, there was plenty to do, see, and learn in the Great Place. Mandela made a firm and lasting friendship with Justice, the Regent's biological son, and the two became inseparable. There was work, as well. Mandela often ironed the Regent's trousers, and the Regent's donning of Western-style clothing made a definite impression on him. Throughout life, Mandela would be a "clothes-horse," proud of his appearance.

Mandela was also able to witness his adopted father's style of government. Jongintaba was not king of the Thembu tribe, but rather the regent, governing the tribe until a young relative came of age. In his autobiography, Mandela described Jongintaba's style of holding a tribal council; there is little doubt that this became the model for much of Mandela's later political style.

> Everyone who wished to speak did so. It was democracy in its purest form. There may have been a hierarchy of importance among the speakers, but everyone was heard, chief and subject, warrior and medicine man, shopkeeper and farmer, landowner and laborer. Only at the end of the meeting, as the sun was setting, would the regent speak. His purpose was to sum up what had been said and form some consensus among the diverse opinions. If no agreement could be reached, another meeting would be held.[6]

Mandela later recalled the Regent's description of himself: "He is like a shepherd. He stays behind the flock, letting the most nimble go out ahead, whereupon the others follow, not realizing that all along they are being directed from behind."[7] Throughout life, Mandela would adhere to the African principle of tribal consensus. Unlike Western democracy, which depends on majority rule, African tribal government depended on agreement by virtually everyone, no matter how long it took to reach it.

MANDELA'S HIGHER EDUCATION

By age 16, Mandela had begun school in earnest. The Regent was proud of both his sons, and expected Justice would one day succeed him and that Mandela would be Justice's chief counselor. This type of kinship arrangement was very common in tribal government.

Justice was four years older, so Mandela attended schools in his adopted brother's wake. Mandela went first to Clarkebury Boarding Institute, then to Healdtown, a Wesleyan college, and finally to the University of Fort Hare. This was the only institution of higher education in all South Africa to which blacks were admitted, and few of the professors realized they were nurturing what might one day become a group of revolutionary leaders.

Mandela did well in his studies. He also picked up habits and attitudes that would last a lifetime. At Clarkebury, he developed a love for gardening that became his greatest source of happiness throughout the storms of adult life; at Healdtown, he stood out as a long-distance runner; and at Fort Hare he participated in drama and debate. On one occasion, he acted the part of John Wilkes Booth in a play about Abraham Lincoln.

Mandela also developed his interest in British law. Like most of the students at Fort Hare, he admired many aspects of Great Britain, which had pioneered the way in constitutional democracy and equality before the law. Growing up in South Africa, it was hard not to notice the power of Great Britain, which extended to this African region, so far from the British homeland. Mandela began to aspire to a place in the South African civil service, which was run on British principles.

Mandela's adopted brother Justice did not attend Fort Hare with him, so Mandela turned to his nephew, Kaiser Matanzima, whom everyone called "K.D.," for friendship. The two young men would know each other for the rest of their lives. Without K.D., Mandela would have been both lonely and poor, for the Regent did not believe in handing allowances to his children at school. Matanzima shared both money and food with Mandela.

As things turned out, food became an increasingly important issue. Neither Mandela nor K.D. had grown up amidst plenty; both had known times when they had to tighten their stomachs and go without. When tribal Africans had food, though, they prepared it with great care and attention, turning out fine meals. This was not the case at Fort Hare, and early in 1941, Mandela and about 25 other students signed an official protest against the food that was being served.

The issue grew to where it threatened the integrity of the college. Dr. Alexander Kerr, the school president, persuaded virtually all of the 25 signers to withdraw their names from the petition, but he could not win over Mandela. When the young African refused to withdraw his name, Dr. Kerr calmly said he should go home when the winter semester ended, but that he could return in the fall if he would withdraw his name. Mandela explained:

> Something inside me would not let me. While I appreciated Dr. Kerr's position and his willingness to give me another chance, I resented his absolute power over my fate. I should have had every right to resign from the SRC [Student's Representative Council] if I wished. This injustice rankled, and at that moment I saw Dr. Kerr less as a benefactor than as a not-altogether-benign dictator.[8]

Mandela went home to the Great Place.

The Regent Jongintaba was furious with his adopted son. Of course Nelson would withdraw his name and end the protest. Of course he would return to the college that autumn. Then the Regent made another pronouncement. He said he was feeling poorly and believed he had not long to live. It was his duty to arrange marriages for both his sons, so he could leave them in a settled state. Therefore he had gone ahead and arranged marriages that should be performed that summer. Mandela and Justice would have none of it.

They were still tribal Africans, and everyone expected them to obey the Regent, but the two young men had been away at school long enough to realize there was a big world waiting for them, even grander than the Great Place. They had picked up enough Western ideas about individuality and personal choice to want to select their own wives. So, they ran away.

CHAPTER 3

The City
of Gold

Justice and Mandela ran away in the spring of 1941. Mandela was 22 and Justice was about 26. They escaped from the Transkei and found their way by automobile to eGoli (in Zulu, "City of Gold"). The whites called it Johannesburg.

The greatest gold strike in world history happened at Johannesburg in 1886. Until then, the town had been a very small place, but in the wake of the gold discovery, Johannesburg became one of the great cities of all Africa, and later of the entire world. Thousands, then hundreds of thousands, came to Johannesburg, hoping to win riches and fame in its gold and diamond pits. Most were disappointed.

Johannesburg had more gold than any other place on Earth, but the early miners found and claimed the best spots. Many of these early miners later formed companies that were able to make fortunes extracting mineral wealth from the soil, but little of this money trickled down to the average miner or goldseeker.

Enough time had passed that Justice and Mandela did not expect to find gold. Rather, they hoped to work in the mines, as did

Deemed the City of Gold because of its multitude of gold mines, Johannesburg, South Africa, drew Mandela when he was a young man searching for work. This 1940 photograph depicts Rissik Street in downtown Johannesburg.

many migrant black Africans. From childhood, both Mandela and Justice had listened with rapt attention to the occasional black African back from the mines. Perhaps to make their back-breaking labor more bearable, the black miners exaggerated the fun and good times; they did not tell the boys they slept on tiny cots in hot and humid places. Nor did they describe the continuing segregation between the races. The word *apartheid* was not used much in the 1930s, but it would be employed on a more constant basis through the 1940s. Two British travelers described Johannesburg in the 1970s, three decades after Mandela and Justice arrived:

> Whatever people do here, it is not far removed from gold. Nearly two million live in Johannesburg. They live off gold or the life it generates—more than 400,000 work in the mines themselves. They dig gold, refine it, shape it, eat it, sleep it, buy and sell it; every business is linked, however indirectly, with it.[9]

Mandela and Justice arrived in 1941, eager to make their mark.

Tribal agents in the city quickly arranged for work for Justice, but they had heard nothing of Mandela. His first work was as a night watchman. Carrying a big stick, he stood in front of a mine entrance, near a sign that proclaimed "Natives cross here." A few months passed before Mandela found his bearings. The great city, with its electric lights, streetcars, automobiles, and endless lines of paved road must have been quite overwhelming to a young man from the Transkei. He could easily have been swallowed up by the big city and could have been one of the many early failures, were it not for another Transkei native.

Walter Sisulu's father was white and his mother was black. He had grown up in the Transkei but came to Johannesburg at an early age and found his way in the world of the whites. Asking for help, Mandela was directed to Walter Sisulu's office, where the two men met for the first time. Theirs would be a lifetime friendship. Sisulu later recalled that he saw a tall, slim young man of undeniable courage and ability: He just needed a chance. Sisulu led Mandela to the real estate offices of Lazar Sidelsky, where Mandela was soon employed as a clerk. This was no small achievement. Such jobs nearly always went to whites.

Knowing he was fortunate, Mandela settled down to life in the big city. He took law classes in the evenings, worked at the real estate office during the day, and went to as many parties as he could. The black townships surrounding Johannesburg were poor, but they boasted a vibrant night life, with aspiring musicians, lawyers, and athletes all jumbled together. Life was not easy, however. Mandela often went a day or two without anything to eat, and he frequently walked nine miles a day to save train fare. These early days of hardship fashioned him into a powerful young man, though—full of vim, vigor, and determination.

THE WHEEL OF FORTUNE

Mandela arrived in Johannesburg in 1941, the year the United States entered World War II. South Africa was already in the war, having entered as a British ally in 1939. This action was not universally popular. Many Afrikaners resented any connection with Great Britain, and some Afrikaners openly sympathized with Nazi Germany. Mandela and his circle of friends paid some attention to the war, especially because of the contribution by black Africans. More than 100,000 blacks served in the South African army, and many won marks of distinction in combat. Mandela and other blacks believed this participation would enhance blacks' status in South Africa, but they were wrong.

White South Africans actually turned *against* black South Africans because of their participation in the war. Many white South Africans viewed black involvement in politics or the military as a serious threat, and by the time World War II ended in 1945, a backlash against black South Africans was in the wings. Mandela did not know this, however; he was far too busy building his life.

Late in 1941, the year he and Justice ran away, Mandela received a visit from his adoptive father, Jongintaba. The Regent came to Johannesburg to see both his sons. Visibly aged, the

Mandela's First Marriage

It may seem odd to put Mandela's first marriage into a separate section, but in some way this reflects his life. Mandela and Evelyn Ntoko Mase seemed well suited, but it may have always been an appearance. They soon had three children, whom Mandela loved to bathe and read stories to, but his activities as a lawyer, and then as a revolutionary, always came first.

Mandela, Evelyn, and their children lived in difficult circumstances until they found a home at 8115 Orlando. Orlando was the name of the township they lived in. Houses throughout the townships were numbered, rather than having street names. Evelyn thought of her husband as a terrific student, who would become a terrific lawyer, but she was appalled as he drifted into politics and later into revolutionary activity.

By the early 1950s, the couple was seriously estranged. Mandela spent most of his time out of the house. The presence of their three children made it seem as if this was a happy and engaged family, but in fact, appearances lied. Mandela and Evelyn were deeply unhappy. In 1957, Mandela was introduced to the woman who became the great love of his life. He fell in love with Nomzamo Winnifred ("Winnie") Madikizela and quickly set about divorcing Evelyn. Nelson and Winnie married in 1958. After this, Mandela and Evelyn had little contact. Only when their oldest son, Thembi, died in 1966 did Mandela send his former wife a letter.

Regent politely inquired into Mandela's living conditions and prospects, but did not say one word about Mandela having run away from home. As was the case with leaving his mother, Mandela had experienced a complete break when he made his move. Though he had fond feelings toward the Regent, he knew he would never return to the Transkei, that he would not trade his new life in the big city to return to the country. The Regent died in 1942, and his son, Justice, returned to the Transkei to take his place. Mandela was now completely on his own, and doing rather well.

Mandela was proficient as a clerk in the real estate firm, and he was pursuing a law degree through night school. He frequented the home of Walter Sisulu, where he met a charming young nurse. Evelyn Ntoko Mase was also from the Transkei. The two were married in 1943. In the meanwhile, Mandela began to drift into politics. Later, he expressed the situation like this:

> I cannot pinpoint a moment when I became politicized, when I knew that I would spend my life in the liberation struggle. To be an African in South Africa means that one is politicized from the moment of one's birth, whether one acknowledges it or not. An African child is born in an Africans Only hospital, taken home in an Africans Only bus, lives in an Africans Only area, and attends Africans Only schools, if he attends school at all.[10]

Still, it seems possible that a bus strike played a role.

In 1943, the year Mandela married Evelyn, the train companies in Johannesburg announced a fare increase from five to six pennies per ride. This 20 percent increase was a severe hardship to many people, but especially so for Africans who lived in the outer townships of Orlando, Soweto, and others. For about 10 days, black South Africans carried out a bus and train strike,

General Jan Christiaan Smuts led the Afrikaner forces during the Anglo-Boer War, but later he became an advocate of British policies. He led the country into World War II as prime minister of the white South African government, but was ousted from office in 1948 when the National Party became the ruling body.

choosing to walk very long distances to and from work. The collective action worked; the train company brought the fare back to five pennies per ride. For the first time in living memory, black South Africans had carried out a successful boycott and made a major white company change its policy. Mandela now joined the African National Congress.

Years passed—years in which Mandela earned his law degree and his children passed from toddlers to young children. Mandela was not outwardly political in these years, but he had hundreds of conversations with men who were, and, to his own surprise, some of his prejudices were breaking down.

Often we think of prejudice as a one-way street, but in Mandela's life it was more like an equal opportunity employer. Having grown up exclusively among blacks, and living in the black townships around Johannesburg, Mandela was biased against whites, Communists, Indians, and coloreds. These prejudices broke down rather slowly over the years, and might have never broken down had he not entered into so many political conversations.

Though he was decidedly against communism, Mandela found many communists to be earnest, thoughtful, and sincere people. Though he distrusted the potential influence of Indians in the African National Congress, he admitted they made some of the most articulate and committed members. His prejudice against coloreds (the term for people of mixed race in South Africa) took longer to evaporate, because he met few of them in the townships. This aspect of his learning came later.

THE OUTSIDE WORLD

There was much reason for hope, even optimism. The end of World War II showed the horrible reality behind the face of fascism. It seemed unlikely anyone would be attracted to such a program in the future.

Though U.S. President Franklin D. Roosevelt was dead and U.K. Prime Minister Winston Churchill was out of office, the two men had written many statements together, including the Atlantic Charter of 1941, which spoke of freedom and choice for people around the world. Mandela remembered the positive aspects of his British-influenced education and hoped the concept of fair play would soon come to South Africa.

Liberation movements were succeeding globally. In 1947, the Republic of India was born. Mohandas Gandhi, who had spent 20 years of his life in South Africa, became the president of the new republic. Although he was assassinated in 1948, the mere presence of a free India encouraged many South Africans.

In 1948, Israel was born. The Jewish people had been without a homeland since the Romans destroyed Jerusalem in A.D. 70. Now, largely as the result of action by the United Nations, Israel became a new nation. In that same year, however, a time when the tide of progress was high, South Africa turned its back on liberalism and progressivism.

Until 1948, the white South African government had been run by the well-meaning, though patronizing, Prime Minister Jan Christiaan Smuts. Much earlier in life, Smuts had been an Afrikaner general during the Anglo-Boer War, but once that conflict was over, he reconciled with the British and became one of their strongest advocates. Smuts played a leading role in prompting South Africa to enter World War II. He was also one of the authors of the new United Nations Charter. Smuts was swept aside, however, by the National Party, which won the elections of 1948.

The National Party (almost synonymous with the Afrikaners) campaigned on the platform of fighting what it called the Black Peril. It was obvious that the black population of South Africa was growing much faster than the British or Afrikaner populace, and the National Party called for strict separation between the races. One of their slogans was "the Kaffir in his place." (*Kaffir* is an Arabic word for "infidel"; whites called South African blacks Kaffirs for generations.) Mandela, his friends, and the African National Congress were about to confront one of the great evils of modern times: apartheid.

CHAPTER 4

Marriage, Family, and Tragedy

B y 1950, Nelson Mandela was one of the leaders of the African National Congress. He had his law degree and was soon to open one of the few black law offices in South Africa. Like many of his countrymen, however, he was disturbed and distressed by what he saw.

The National Party won the 1948 elections and proceeded to establish apartheid on a grand scale. Many white South Africans had believed in the idea of apartheid before this, but now they set about putting their ideas into practice. Laws were passed in 1950 that forbade marriage between whites and blacks. These laws were expanded to include intermarriage between any of the four official racial groups: whites, blacks, Indians, and coloreds. There had never been many marriages between the different racial groups, but the official declaration that it was forbidden naturally caused a storm of protest. Worse followed.

Whites had always held most of the jobs in business, banking, transportation, and the like. Blacks had traditionally only had access to low-paying jobs. Now, however, it became official policy to ensure that blacks only came to the cities for a short time and that they were then rotated back to their tribal farmlands. The intention was to create a temporary workforce of low-paid laborers, who could not organize and fight for better wages, since they would be replaced on a regular, ongoing basis.

The pass system, which restricted the movements of Africans around South Africa by forcing them to show passbooks, was always difficult, but it became more onerous after the 1948 elections. Mandela and other leaders of the African National Congress were regularly prevented from leaving Johannesburg.

All these restrictions were bad enough. The breaking point came when the white Afrikaner government announced its intention to take over Sophiatown. One of the numerous black townships ringed about Johannesburg, Sophiatown was no great prize, materially speaking, but it was a cultural center for blacks, and many had made their homes and lives there. Now, for purely racial reasons, the Afrikaner government planned to destroy the old settlement town and replace it with modern suburbs.

The drive to reduce Sophiatown neatly coincided with South Africa's 300th birthday. In the spring of 1652, the Afrikaner government announced its intention to celebrate the anniversary of Dutch settlers landing at Cape Town in 1652. Though the precise date of their landing was not verified, the celebrations were held on April 6, 1952.

Just weeks before the 300th anniversary, the highest court in South Africa declared that several of the new apartheid laws were unconstitutional. Many blacks hoped this was the beginning of a break in the logjam of apartheid, but they were mistaken. Afrikaner leaders replied swiftly by passing a law that made the South African legislature the highest law in the land, higher than the court. Thus the apartheid laws remained on the books and in effect.

The year 1952 was a big one for Nelson Mandela. In June, he was one of the key leaders of a series of protests against the

South Africans, as shown in this photo from the early 1950s, take to the streets to protest the oppressive minority government. Whatever freedoms Africans had were abolished with the establishment of the new apartheid regime.

government's apartheid policy. These nonviolent demonstrations appeared to be successful; thousands of people eagerly signed up to join the African National Congress. Later that year, Mandela and his friend Oliver Tambo opened Mandela & Tambo, one of the few Johannesburg law firms to serve blacks and the only all-black law firm in South Africa.

Mandela became more of a presence than ever. Now in his mid-30s, he was a large, handsome man who delighted in his

Oldsmobile, his sharp business suits, and in looking the part of a solid citizen. At the same time, he was more committed than ever to fighting racial injustice. Mandela & Tambo took on nearly all the major legal actions brought by the African National Congress. Mandela was also busy helping young black people who had arrived recently in the city, much as Walter Sisulu had helped him in 1941.

Mandela, Tambo, Sisulu, and other leaders of the African National Congress fought the attempt to remove people from Sophiatown. They failed, and by 1953 the black township had been leveled to make room for Afrikaner housing developments. The contrast between black townships and white suburbs could not have been more striking. The former were culturally alive and vital, but materially they were depressed slums. The latter had swimming pools, social clubs, and the like. Mandela discussed his thoughts at the time:

> The lesson I took away from the campaign was that in the end, we had no alternative to armed and violent resistance. Over and over again, we had used all the nonviolent weapons in our arsenal—speeches, deputations, threats, marches, strikes, stay-aways, voluntary imprisonment—all to no avail, for whatever we did was met by an iron hand. A freedom fighter learns the hard way that it is the oppressor who defines the nature of the struggle, and the oppressed [are] often left no recourse but to use methods that mirror those of the oppressor. At a certain point, one can only fight fire with fire.[11]

Mandela had become a revolutionary.

The mid-1950s were not promising times for revolutionaries. The Soviet Union crushed a Hungarian revolution. The Cold War continued to dominate the headlines. Oppressive regimes continued to rule in Cuba, the Philippines, and elsewhere. Surveying the global scene, there was little reason for optimism, so Mandela and his comrades looked to their own African traditions. In 1955, they drew up the Freedom Charter of the African National Congress (ANC):

> We, the people of South Africa, declare for all our country and the world to know:
>
> That South Africa belongs to all who live in it, black and white, and that no government can justly claim authority unless it is based on the will of the people;
>
> That our people have been robbed of their birthright to land, liberty and peace by a form of government founded on injustice and inequality;
>
> That our government will never be prosperous or free until all our people live in brotherhood, enjoying equal rights and opportunities.[12]

Anyone who read the Freedom Charter in full would have been satisfied that the demands were reasonable ones, but there were some sentences concerning property and the wealth of the nation that made many people think the ANC leaders were Communists. This suspicion helped the Afrikaner government mobilize energy and force against Mandela and the ANC. The world was then in the midst of the Cold War between the capitalist United States and Communist Soviet Union. Where one stood on matters of private property was of great importance, and Mandela and the ANC may have hurt themselves through their statements on the matter.

TRIAL AND DELIGHT

In 1957, Mandela and 28 other ANC members went on trial. They were accused of treason. During the long trial, Mandela emerged as the best-dressed man in the courtroom. He favored snappy suits and his flashing smile drew attention wherever he was. As he neared his fortieth birthday, Mandela was very much a man on the make, as well as a revolutionary. Yet, in the midst of all the

After a four-and-a-half year trial, Mandela and other revolutionaries were acquitted of accounts of treason in 1961. He stands here, center right, at the beginning of the trial, singing with those who shared his vision of abolishing apartheid rule.

chaos and uproar, he found time for a new relationship, and then a new wife.

Mandela and his wife, Evelyn, were estranged by 1957. Perhaps they remained together for their three children—oldest son, Thembi, son Makgatho, and daughter Maki (Makaziwe)—but one could also argue that the parents were not together at all. Mandela stayed away from home as often as he could, and with his law practice and defending himself in the treason trial, he was busy indeed. On the rare occasions when he was home, his bright cheerfulness seemed dimmed. He and Evelyn were a very unhappy couple.

Evelyn had always believed Mandela would outgrow his revolutionary aspirations. To her, it was quite enough that her husband was a well-respected attorney. She thought he should perform his legal work and advance the cause of their children

A glowing Mandela stands with his young bride, Winnie, on their wedding day in 1958. Though at first she seemed complacent about Mandela's revolutionary undertakings, Winnie later took on more conspicuous roles that championed Mandela's actions for freedom.

rather than act on behalf of millions of others he had never met. Mandela's mother, who got along well with Evelyn, felt much the same way. Whether the marriage might have continued was a moot point from the moment Mandela met Winnie Madikizela.

If there is such a thing as love at first sight, it probably is much rarer than people wish to believe. It does happen sometimes, though, and the meeting between Mandela and Winnie was clearly one of those moments. She was from the Transkei, and she knew the name Mandela long before she moved to Johannesburg. Winnie was a striking 22-year-old when she met the 39-year-old Mandela. He fell in love with her at once.

They met over a legal matter, but he took her out the next day, and the rest is history. From the beginning, they were a striking and passionate couple, holding hands, gazing adoringly at each other in public. Perhaps he was more smitten with her than vice versa, and perhaps she fell more in love with his fame than the man himself, but there is no denying they found great happiness together.

Once he met Winnie, Mandela initiated divorce proceedings against Evelyn. He showed no remorse over the breakup of his marriage, but it would haunt him for years to come. His son Thembi was never reconciled to the divorce, and the relationship between father and son, which had previously been warm and open, turned sour.

Mandela and Winnie were married in June 1958. This was one of the most public and joyful events of Mandela's life. He wore white gloves to the wedding, and his exuberance was palpable. He was starting life over again. He had started over two or three times before; first when he left Qunu; second when he left the Great Place for Johannesburg; and now when he married Winnie. Though he claimed to hate change, Mandela was by now practiced at the art of making a break with the past and moving on.

The wedding day was marred in one respect. Because of the ban placed on him, Mandela had to head back to Johannesburg before dark. There was not time enough to cut the wedding cake, so Winnie saved it and later said there was a piece of cake still waiting to be eaten. Years later, in 1988, it was destroyed in a household fire.

Winnie Mandela had married the most famous black man in South Africa. He had married a gorgeous young woman, who, at first, shared none of his revolutionary fervor. Winnie did not resent or resist her husband's revolutionary actions, however: far from it. She was young, though, and it took some time for her to catch up with all the years of education and development that had produced Mandela and the African National Congress. Some of his comrades thought he made a mistake in marrying Winnie, but later they would witness her coming into her own as a revolutionary.

For her part, Winnie stuck bravely to a man and a cause she had come to know very quickly. Mandela came home tired from the law office each day, but he was then almost always besieged by African National Congress members wanting to discuss strategies. "Even at that stage, life with him was a life without him. He did not ever pretend that I would have some special claim to his time," Winnie explained.[13]

SPLIT IN THE RANKS OF THE ANTI-APARTHEID MOVEMENT

The year 1958 could have been a time of real celebration for the ANC. The Afrikaner government dropped the charges

In the Black Townships

Americans watching television in 1976 were shocked at the images of violence in Soweto, South Africa. Small children and teenagers scrambled for cover as police opened fire with real bullets as well as tear gas. This was when most Americans came to know something about South Africa's black townships.

South Africa was predominantly rural until the 1880s. The gold strikes of that decade changed everything. Millions of people moved into the cities of Johannesburg, Pretoria, Cape Town, and Durban. Most of the first arrivals were white, and they set up their homes in the central part of these cities.

Blacks, Indians, and coloreds came later. They found the best land and space already taken up. Moreover, there was already a racial prejudice, which only grew worse with time. Indians and coloreds sometimes managed to live in near-equality with whites, but blacks, shut out of the nicer neighborhoods, ended up in the townships that came to surround each of the major cities. Soweto (which means the "southwestern townships") was only the best-known of dozens of such places. Mandela arrived against 131 of the accused, though Mandela, Oliver Tambo, and Albert Luthuli were among the remaining 95 indicted. The African National Congress now faced an internal crisis, however.

A growing number of ANC members called for a strictly Africanist approach to freedom. They pointed out that the ANC was composed of blacks, Indians, and coloreds, whereas independence movements in other countries were restricted to black natives. Mandela, Luthuli, Tambo, and others felt this was too limited a platform from which to operate, and they were appalled when many ANC members dropped out and created their own Pan-Africanist Congress, in 1959. A weakened ANC returned to the treason trial in 1960.

in 1941, when the townships were nearly bursting because of population increase.

A comparison can be made between places like Soweto in South Africa and places like Harlem in the United States. Both places were distinctly black in population and culture, but the comparison is not complete until one points out that Soweto and other townships often lacked electricity and had a bare minimum of running water. Black South Africans did the best they could, and the townships often became centers of vibrant music, poetry, and celebration. But anyone who visited the white suburbs just a few miles away was shocked by the difference.

Mandela lived in the Alexandra township when he first arrived, but he settled in Orlando township with his first wife, Evelyn. Years later, he claimed he had felt more comfortable in the former, saying that in Alexandra he had a home without a house, and that in Orlando he had a house but lacked a real home. Even Mandela did not foresee the violence that would break out in the townships in the 1970s and 1980s. By then, he was locked away in prison, but many people chanted his name as they protested and rioted in the streets.

THE SHARPEVILLE MASSACRE

The treason trial had lasted so long that it had ceased to be sensational. Even Mandela, who still sparkled in his freshly pressed suits, was often found reading the newspaper during the long court sessions. There was pressure mounting, though—pressure from inside and out.

The black townships were close to a state of revolution. For the past decade, people in the townships had listened to leaders like Mandela, Tambo, Sisulu, and others. They believed the time for action had come. Meanwhile, the Afrikaner government thought the same thing. White government officials had investigated Mandela and the ANC for a long time, and they were convinced most ANC members were communists at heart. This added a second weapon with which to attack the ANC, for white South Africans were virulently anticommunist. Both sides laid their plans.

In the spring of 1960, there was a great black movement in the townships around Johannesburg, Pretoria, and Cape Town. This was the first time black agitators had struck in all three places at once. Violence was narrowly averted in Cape Town, but disaster struck in the township of Sharpeville. Police opened fire on demonstrators; 67 people were killed.

Television had come to American homes in the 1950s and was spreading to South African homes, as well. Millions of Americans watched news footage of the Sharpeville killings, and were appalled to learn of conditions for black South Africans. Given that America was embroiled in its own civil rights movement, launched by Martin Luther King, Jr., and others, Americans became keenly interested in South Africa.

Sharpeville was the end of the line for nonviolent resistance. Mandela and his comrades stood by nonviolent methods throughout the 1950s, but they were now ready to take up the gun. At the same time, the Afrikaner government also upped the stakes. Not only were police and soldiers called in to meet every protest demonstration, but the Afrikaner government announced its intention to leave the British Commonwealth of Nations.

This was a momentous step. South African whites had a mixed heritage, coming from both the Netherlands and Great Britain. One reason Mandela and others had believed nonviolence would work was their training in the British concepts of fair play and equality before the law. If South Africa left the Commonwealth, though, it would effectively turn its back on British traditions.

The British government was displeased, to say the least. British Prime Minister Harold Wilson had made a trip to South Africa just a few months earlier, proclaiming that the winds of change were about to reach all through the continent, but he had not wanted to provoke South Africa into leaving the Commonwealth. The Afrikaner government took the big leap. In May 1961, South Africa became a republic, completely separate from Great Britain. What little restraint there had been on the Afrikaner government was now completely gone.

CHAPTER 5

In Castro's Image

Few people today associate Nelson Mandela with Fidel Castro of Cuba. The former seems so clearly to be a success story, whereas the latter evokes the image of a bitter hanger-on from former times. In the early 1960s, however, Mandela and his comrades admired Fidel Castro and hoped his brand of popular revolution could be transplanted to South Africa.

In 1960, the ANC created a new branch of its leadership. This branch, called the Spear of the Nation, was headed by Nelson Mandela. Though he had spent his adult life as a man of peace, law, and civil justice, Nelson Mandela was keenly aware of his black tribal heritage. He was the great-grandson of a king, and his ancestors had fought the British and Afrikaners with equal fury. Now, at the age of 42, he began to see himself as a violent revolutionary.

Aware of the change, the Afrikaner government tried to have Mandela arrested. He went underground, however, and soon became adept at making and changing disguises. Sometimes he was a cab driver; at other times he was a miner or laborer. There is little doubt Mandela enjoyed the role. He was a very physical man and had increased his strength through boxing in the 1950s. He liked being on the run, in a romantic sense, even though it separated him from Winnie and their two children.

Winnie by now had become a revolutionary herself. Tall and strong, she stood in the way of the police, who often raided her family home, and on one occasion she knocked a policeman flat. Winnie and Mandela arranged many secret meetings, during which their joy was great, but these were merely interludes, lasting only a few hours. Deep in her heart, Winnie must have known that her chances of seeing Mandela as a free man, living in the open, were small.

In 1961, Mandela went on a tour of several African and European nations. He snuck out of South Africa and visited Algeria and Morocco. There he learned how to fire a gun, and he practiced his marksmanship.

Mandela and his fellows were inspired by the success of Fidel Castro and Ernesto "Che" Guevara. The two men and their guerrilla army had overthrown the corrupt Batista regime in Cuba in 1959 and 1960. With only the slimmest of military means, Guevara and Castro had undermined and then brought down the hated Batista. That Castro was a Communist did not deter Mandela from admiring him. Mandela had come a long way from the young man who detested Indians, coloreds, and Communists. Mandela visited London for a week. He said of his experiences: "I confess to being something of an Anglophile. When I thought of Western democracy and freedom, I thought of the British parliamentary system. In so many ways, the very model of the gentleman for me was an Englishman."[14] Photographs taken of Mandela at this time show a vigorous and determined man. He was at the height of his physical and intellectual powers, and he believed he could be the Fidel Castro of South Africa. He was wrong.

Mandela was essentially a thinker, a feeler, and a doer. Though he had an imposing physique, he was not a rugged revolutionary in the tradition of Castro and Guevara. Rather,

Fidel Castro's revolutionary spirit was an inspiration to Mandela. Castro, pictured here at center right, and co-revolutionary Che Guevara brought down the corrupt and feared Batista regime of Cuba in 1959 and 1960. Mandela likened the act to his own efforts at political revolution.

he was an adapter, someone who tried, failed, and tried again. He was about to experience one of his greatest moments of failure.

Mandela was captured soon after he returned to South Africa. Ever since 1962, there have been suspicions that the U.S. Central Intelligence Agency (CIA) fed information to South Africa's government, helping it capture Mandela. These suspicions have never been proved, but it is true that the U.S. government saw Mandela and other black activists as dangers during the Cold War. In any event, Mandela was captured.

First, Mandela was held in a jail at Pretoria. Then he and about 10 other political prisoners were taken on a 1,000-mile van ride, culminating at Cape Town. From here there was only one destination: The Island. Robben Island was already semilegendary in South African history. Located off the coast, eight miles from Cape Town, the island is blown by harsh winter winds, and, though it is within sight of the beautiful city, Robben Island is one of the harshest environments to be found. One can compare it with Alcatraz in the United States, or Devil's Island in Guinea. Alcatraz is only half a mile from the mainland, however. The analogy to Devil's Island is closer: Very few prisoners have ever escaped from Devil's Island, and, it is believed, only one man has ever escaped from Robben Island.

Mandela and his fellow prisoners arrived to a chilling reception. Afrikaner guards shouted, "This is the Island! Here you will die!" They made cattle calls, expecting Mandela and the others to run and be herded. Mandela would not do this, and soon he met a captain of the guard, who moved as if to strike him. Summoning all his courage, Mandela said he would sue the captain and make him as poor as a church mouse if he struck him once. Astonished by this resistance, the captain laid off, for the moment.[15] But there was no doubt: Mandela was in jail.

Mandela was not well suited to prison life. Vigorous and active throughout life, he was now deprived of his early morning exercise, one of the keystones of his day. Things became worse when the Afrikaner government found and raided a secret hide-away of the ANC leaders. Documents were found that incriminated most of the ANC leaders, including Mandela. Even if the ANC had

Influences on the Peacemaker

Mandela's father died when he was young, so Mandela did not have the time to imitate his father's style of leadership, but stubbornness was very likely part of what he inherited from this parent. Mandela's father was deprived of his tribal leadership because of a conflict with a British magistrate. The father would not back down: neither would the son.

After his father died, the Regent of the Tembu people, Jongin-taba, was Mandela's surrogate father for many years; he had a leadership style that was both apparent and could be consciously imitated. Mandela noticed early on that the Regent prided himself in matters of clothing and dress. Though he was a tribal African leader, the Regent wore smart-looking Western-style clothes that young Mandela often pressed and ironed. Mandela adopted this charac-teristic, one that would persist throughout his life. During the 1956 treason trial, Mandela was often described as the best-dressed man at his own trial.

More important, though, was the Regent's style of governance. Tribal meetings were held on a regular basis, and there was abso-lutely no sense of hurry in the proceedings. The Regent would say little during the long day of petitions, proposals, and counter-proposals. Only at sundown, when everyone else was weary from the effort of argument and speech-making, did the Regent give an extended talk—and he summarized what he had heard rather than put an official stamp on what had taken place. The Regent had great power within the tribe, but he saw his power as enhanced through consensus, rather than forcing through an opinion. One can certainly say that this was a counterpoint to the stubbornness that Mandela had learned from his father, but, in fact, the two worked together very well. Throughout his long life, Mandela would resist the attempts of others to impose their will on him and on his people, and

not been all that effective and had not harmed many people in its efforts at sabotage, the motive was clearly there. After only a few months at the Island, Mandela and his fellows were brought back to jail in Pretoria to stand trial for a second time.

at the same time he would try to be a benevolent leader himself—one who listened more than he spoke, and one who considered everything before he took action.

The third great influence on Mandela, in both substance and in style, was Chief Albert Luthuli of the Zulu tribe. He was the first African ever to win the Nobel Peace Prize, and also the first black person ever to do so, followed by Martin Luther King Jr. and Nelson Mandela. Born in what was then Rhodesia (now Zimbabwe), Chief Luthuli was powerfully influenced by Christian missionaries in his youth. A devout Christian, Luthuli became first a tribal chief in 1936 and then the president-general of the African National Congress (ANC) in 1952. He and Mandela met many times, and it is likely that Mandela observed the great chief and patterned his policy of slow, incremental development after him. There was some conflict between the two, though. In 1962, for instance, Chief Luthuli demanded to know why he had been left out of the ANC decision-making process that created the Spear of the Nation (the guerrilla branch of the ANC). Luthuli was a great believer in nonviolence, and the new movement distressed him. Mandela explained that he and other leaders of Spear of the Nation had kept Luthuli out of the loop in order to protect him, the recent winner of the Nobel Peace Prize, from controversy.

Finally, there was Walter Sisulu. Mandela and Sisulu started in the relationship of student and tutor, with the older Sisulu taking the lead. Later on, when they spent years together on Robben Island, Mandela was the leader of the imprisoned men, but Sisulu remained his mentor in many ways. Their relationship was long-lasting and encompassed so many varieties of give and take that it is difficult to overestimate how important Walter Sisulu was to Nelson Mandela.

The treason trial dragged on for more than a year. Mandela and his codefendants admitted to many of the charges but insisted they had never attempted violence against people, only government installations. Mandela often entered the courtroom in traditional African dress. He usually held up a clenched fist and the crowd would call out *Amandla!* ("Strength!"). Winnie Mandela made many appearances at court. A striking figure in her own right, Winnie was courted by the press and abhorred by the South African police.

The trial finally ended in June 1964. Mandela's sentencing coincided with the brief time Martin Luther King Jr. spent in the St. Augustine jail. At almost the same moment that the U.S. Senate consented to the Civil Rights Act of 1964, Nelson Mandela and eight other men were sentenced to life in prison. This was a lighter sentence than many had expected. Judge de Wet had the authority to sentence these men to death, but he was not convinced by all aspects of the government's case. Mandela was prepared to die. He left a short list of notes of what he intended to say if he received the death sentence:

1. Statement from dock.
2. I meant everything I said.
3. The blood of many patriots in this country has been shed for demanding treatment in conformity with civilized standards.
4. [A short note, written in Mandela's hand, was undecipherable.]
5. If I must die, let me declare for all to know that I will meet my fate like a man.[16]

Mandela and his codefendants had already agreed not to ask for an appeal. If they received the death sentence, they were ready to die for their cause. If they received life in prison, they would accept that, too. Just days after the sentencing, Mandela returned to Robben Island. This time he remained a very long time.

Mandela gestures while talking to his loyal friend and mentor Walter Sisulu. At the time of this photo in 1965, the two were serving life sentences in the maximum security prison at Robben Island for their attempts to overthrow the white minority government.

COMRADES ON ROBBEN ISLAND

Mandela had several good friends with him on Robben Island. One was Walter Sisulu. Ever since they first met in 1941, the two men had been good friends and close political allies. Sisulu remained Mandela's mentor in many ways.

Oliver Tambo, Mandela's law partner, was not on the prison island. He had left South Africa a few years earlier and was living in London, functioning as the international arm of the African National Congress.

The Afrikaner government thought keeping all the political prisoners in one close group was best: cooped up in one place, these men could not spread their infectious ideas around other parts of the prison and country. There was some truth to the idea, but Mandela later claimed that it was a big mistake; kept together in one prison, the political prisoners reinforced each others' commitment and will.

Prison routine was painful, harsh, and sometimes truly awful. Mandela and his comrades were held in one section of the prison. Each man had his own cell, built bunker-style of reinforced concrete. A solitary 40-watt light bulb gave some comfort in the evening, but the prison guards refused to turn it off at night, and one had to find sleep despite the disturbance of light.

Prisoners were awakened very early. Harsh sounds jarred them from sleep as Afrikaner guards hit the floors with their sticks and clubs. A meager breakfast was served, followed by a short period of outdoor exercise. Then it was off to work.

For many months, the prisoners sat in the hot courtyard of the prison, chopping away at blocks of granite and other stones. They slowly pounded the material into dust, something that had no apparent value. South Africa was determined to break the will of its political prisoners.

June and July were the bleakest months on Robben Island. Winter was in the air and the rains were just beginning. It never seemed to go above 40°F. Mandela recounted the experience: "Even in the sun, I shivered in my light khaki shirt. It was then that I first understood the cliché of feeling the cold in one's bones. At noon we would break for lunch. The first week all we were given was soup, which stank horribly."[17] A solitary man might well have despaired and died, but Mandela had the company of his fellow political prisoners. They were often prevented from talking, by the guards, but they used hand signals and gestures. Over time an incredible intimacy built up among the prisoners; they could often understand each other with only a nod or a frown.

Slowly, Mandela and the others began to penetrate the wall of their Afrikaner guards. Though the guards acted very much alike, the prisoners began to perceive small differences. Perhaps one smiled every so often. Perhaps another showed a bit of compassion. This, Mandela later said, was one of the great lessons of his time in prison: that every hurt and pain was administered by fellow humans, who increasingly began to demonstrate differences that their captors could perceive. The worst was yet to come, however.

After several years of splitting stone in the courtyard, Mandela and his fellows were taken, each day, to a limestone quarry. A bus carried them over, and there they spent the better part of the day, hacking away in the limestone pits. Harder work cannot be imagined. The sunlight was blinding, and, as it bounced and reflected off the white limestone, it damaged the prisoners' eyes. They made requests for sunglasses, but several years passed before they received them. Mandela's vision was permanently damaged.

A group of fierce Afrikaner guards tried to keep the prisoners silent while working. Even here, though, there were small breaks in the oppression. Mandela and the others found that some guards were gentler than others, and they managed to sneak in some conversations. Later, as it became obvious the convicts would not escape, some guards stood many yards away and made no attempt to stop the conversations.

Robben Island offered so many hardships and privations that it is easy to forget one of the most important: the lack of contact with one's family. From the moment Mandela was sentenced, Winnie made numerous requests to see him. Because of his classification, Mandela could only have one visit every six months. Winnie had to travel nearly a thousand miles in order to meet him, and even then, her time was limited to half an hour. Mandela described the cruelly brief first meeting:

> The visiting room for noncontact visits was cramped and windowless. . . . One sat in a chair and looked through the thick, smudged glass that has a few small holes drilled into it to permit conversation. One had to talk very loudly to be heard.[18]

That first meeting was awkward and painful. Mandela lamented that Winnie looked so thin and frail and urged her to put on weight. He learned that his mother was not in good health and that his son Thembi was estranged from him. One can only guess at Mandela's pain when the guards abruptly shouted the half hour was up. Was this what Winnie had traveled a thousand miles for?

Mandela's inner strength rarely deserted him. He usually found ways of seeking solace, even in prison; years later, the guards would allow him and others to do some vegetable gardening, which brought great relief. His occasional "noncontact" visits with Winnie, however, often left him drained and depressed. He loved her with all the desperation that lovers can have, yet the closest he could come was looking at her through the thick, smudged glass. Things were about to get even worse.

CHAPTER 6

The Darkest Times

When Mandela and his comrades were put on Robben Island, many white South Africans breathed a great sigh of relief. The major leaders of the African National Congress were either jailed or in exile. At least from the point of view of stability, things should get better; this was not to be, however. Even though South Africa's economy grew at a record pace in the 1960s, the land was troubled. There were no major riots or outbreaks, such as at Sharpeville, but there was plenty of unease.

Prime Minister Hendrik Verwoerd was assassinated in 1966. Verwoerd was the prime architect of apartheid, the man who had envisioned both the philosophy behind the movement and the means to carry it out. Now he was dead, killed by a white message runner in the Parliament building. It made no difference that his assassin was white. Most South Africans immediately blamed Mandela and the other ANC leaders, whether in prison or in exile. Mandela and his fellow prisoners learned of the prime minister's death in a circuitous way, for they received a new chief jailer.

South African Prime Minister Hendrik Verwoerd, the primary architect of apartheid, poses while looking over correspondence in May 1960. A month earlier, Verwoerd narrowly missed death in an attempted assassination. He eventually was assassinated by a white South African in 1966.

Van Rensburg arrived at Robben Island immediately after Verwoerd's assassination. A big, strong, but clumsy man, he had a reputation as one of the worst of all jail administrators. A harsh man with a grating voice, he did everything possible to worsen the lives of the political prisoners. One of the most telling and revolting of the stories is that he chose to urinate near the table where prisoners were served their food.

Mandela and his comrades began calling Van Rensburg "the Suitcase," which referred both to his physical size and the fact that no prisoner would carry his lunch pail. One day Van Rensburg shouted "Who is suitcase?" On learning this was the prisoner's name for him, Van Rensburg said, "My name is not Suitcase, it's

Dik Nek," which meant "Thick Neck" in Afrikaans (the language of the Afrikaners).[19] This brief moment of frivolity was one of the few in those times. Van Rensburg clamped down on the prisoners, revoking privileges wherever they existed and demanding that more rock be broken and more limestone quarried.

The prisoners became adept at gathering news from the outside. Some of the guards were bored and occasionally gave them information. At other times, knowledge was smuggled onto the island using a variety of methods. In the late 1960s, however, the news was nearly all bad.

Chief Albert Luthuli, who had won the Nobel Peace Prize in 1960, died on his Zulu homestead in 1967. Although Mandela was called the Spear of the Nation, even he had deferred to Luthuli on many occasions in the past. It was hard to imagine the African National Congress without this great leader.

Mandela's mother died in 1968. She was nearly 70 and had enjoyed a good life by Xhosa tribal standards, but Mandela felt a great deal of guilt about his lack of care for her in the past decade or so. While he was a Johannesburg lawyer, Mandela had been able to support her from afar, but she had lived a distance from doctors or any sort of modern conveniences. Mandela expressed his ambivalence about this situation:

> But I came back to the same answer. In South Africa, it is hard for a man to ignore the needs of the people, even at the expense of his own family. I had made my choice, and in the end, she had supported it. But that did not lessen the sadness I felt at not being able to make her more comfortable, or the pain of not being able to lay her to rest.[20]

Mandela asked permission for a week away from prison so he might bury his mother, but this request was refused.

Throughout his years in prison, Mandela worried most about his wife. He thought of his children as having the natural resilience of youth, and he was most concerned how Winnie would bear up under the punishment she might receive from the police. Sure enough, the Mandela home at 8115 Orlando was invaded time and again over the years, often in the middle of the night.

Winnie did very well under the circumstances and shielded the children to the best of her ability. In the spring of 1969, however, police and security invaded their home once more: This time, they took Winnie away. She and 23 others were charged under a new law that made it much easier for the police to arrest and detain suspicious persons. Taken to a jail in Pretoria, Winnie endured more than a year and a half of prison, of which there were hundreds of days of solitary confinement. Even hardened criminals often buckle under just a week or 10 days of "solitary," but somehow Winnie held out. She defied her tormentors and was finally released in 1970.

Just two months after Winnie's arrest came the worst blow of all. In July 1969, the same month that American astronauts landed on the moon, Mandela learned that his eldest son, Thembi, had died in a car accident. Thembi had been living 10 miles away, in Cape Town, and had made a deliberate choice not to visit his father over the past five years. Perhaps he was embittered because of his parents' divorce in 1958; no one can be sure of the exact reason. Now, though, Thembi was dead, and Mandela was inconsolable. That night was probably the worst of Mandela's long life:

> I returned to my cell and lay on my bed. I do not know how long I stayed there, but I did not emerge for dinner. Some of the men looked in, but I said nothing. Finally, Walter came to me and knelt beside my bed, and I handed him the telegram. He said nothing but only held my hand.[21]

Mandela asked permission to attend his son's funeral. Though it was only 10 or 12 miles away, permission was refused.

Fortunately, things were about to get better. Conditions on Robben Island improved at the beginning of the 1970s. This was not from a humane impulse on the part of the South African government but from pressure from the international front and from one very courageous member of the South African Parliament, Helen Suzman, who put pressure on the government.

Working hours continued to be long and tedious, but Mandela and his comrades worked out a system whereby they managed to have long conversations, largely uninterrupted by the guards. So long as the quota of limestone was met, the prisoners were able to make their own schedule for a number of hours each day.

Discussions, arguments, and philosophical dialogues all flourished in the windswept limestone quarry. Mandela, Walter Sisulu, and others acted as if they were a debating society, with high standards for proof and certainty. Mandela was not always liked in these debates. He could be touchy, and it was almost impossible to persuade him of another point of view. One of the few "outside" influences that could be brought to bear on Mandela and the other leaders was the poetry of William Shakespeare. Reaching across 350 years and thousands of miles, Shakespeare's words had a power to move men on Robben Island that no government document could rival. Mandela's favorite quotation from Shakespeare was the following:

> Cowards die many times before their deaths;
> The valiant never taste of death but once.
> Of all the wonders that I yet have heard,
> It seems to me most strange that men should fear;
> Seeing that death, a necessary end,
> Will come when it will come.[22]

The monotonous work continued, as did the poetry and philosophy. Mandela, Sisulu, and others also began taking correspondence courses, sometimes from far-off universities. Mandela studied for a second law degree, this time from the University of London.

Mandela kept an active exercise regimen. He ran when possible and did push-ups and chin-ups. This was something he had started in his twenties, but it was fairly unusual for middle-aged South African men. He noticed that the younger prisoners started to watch him; they seemed to decide that if the "old man" could do this, they could, too.

Exercise helped to drain the tension and relax the mind, so Mandela could concentrate on discussions with his fellows and study when he was alone. His dauntless behavior masked some real difficulties, however. He had high blood pressure, which became worse in the 1970s. He nearly lost his eyesight because of the blinding glare from the sun reflecting off the limestone pit. And he sometimes pushed himself too hard physically; he suffered a knee injury that would afflict him for the rest of his life.

Helen Suzman

Helen Suzman was the only member of the Progressive Party in the South African Parliament. Born in 1917, Suzman was the daughter of a Russian Jewish couple. Her mother died when she was born, and Suzman grew up strong-minded and fiercely independent. She married a medical doctor. The couple had two children, and they seemed ready for a comfortable middle-class life.

Suzman ran for Parliament in 1954. To everyone's surprise, she won the election and kept on winning, so that she eventually served for 35 years. For nearly a decade, she

Helen Suzman, the only member of the Progressive Party in the South African Parliament, was a critical force in helping to change the harsh conditions at Robben Island.

In addition, Mandela was the chief spokesperson for the prison inmates. When there was a controversy or when someone was placed in solitary confinement, Mandela was called on to speak for the group as a whole. This was sometimes a pleasure and sometimes an affliction, depending on the attitude of chief administrator or the local warden at the time.

Every one of the inmates fell into despair sometimes, but the good news was that they never all despaired at the same time. Mandela and his fellows became masters, experts really, at detecting slight shifts in mood, among both themselves and those who guarded them. Just as the inmates did not have a uniform response to the situation, so did the guards vary in their attitudes toward the prisoners. From an early age, Mandela had

was the only Progressive in Parliament, and she often endured painful attacks by opposition leaders such as John Vorster and P.W. Botha.

Suzman asked for permission to visit the prisoners on Robben Island. She was the only member of the government to look into matters on the prison island. She arrived in early 1967 and was shocked by the conditions she found there. Mandela told her of one prison guard who had a swastika tattooed on his arm; she worked to have this man removed very quickly.

Years passed before she was able to visit again, however; the white government continually denied her requests. When she returned in 1977, Suzman found the material conditions somewhat better. She later visited Mandela in Pollsmoor Prison, and the two had an emotional reunion at his home in Orlando in 1990.

Suzman was nominated for the Nobel Peace Prize in 1983, though she did not win. She retired from politics in 1989, after creating an enviable legacy. She was one of the tireless advocates for black South Africans who went against the notion that all whites were oppressors.

been taught to look for the good in all people; he now put that into practice, noticing the differences among the guards and sometimes making small progress in human relations with those who showed some humanity.

Then came the first real news from the outside world: Soweto. These townships around Johannesburg had long been a focus of discontent, but the breaking point came when the school authorities announced black children would be instructed in Afrikaans as well as English. In June 1976, the children and teenagers of Soweto rose up in a fury, throwing rocks, mouthing insults, and making life miserable for the police of the townships. The military was called in, and dozens of young people were killed or wounded that month. The most sensational photograph of the time—and the one that sent the news of Soweto around the globe—was of a young black man carrying a 13-year-old boy who had been shot and killed; the boy's sister ran alongside, sobbing. The police and military were able to contain the children and teenagers, but the news was out. People around the world began to learn more about apartheid and the South African government, and international opinion began to turn against the white minority there.

Mandela learned of Soweto weeks later, when the first prisoners began to arrive. Ever since he had arrived in 1964, Mandela had been incarcerated with roughly the same group of men. Most arrived while in their thirties and forties and were older now, but the new inmates were in their teens and twenties, and a real generational conflict began to emerge.

The younger prisoners all knew of Mandela and Sisulu, and the Rivonia Trial of 1964. To these young men, Mandela and his fellows were heroes who had been locked away from the world too long. On arriving at Robben Island, though, many of the young men began to question the wisdom of their elders, especially when it came to making arrangements with the guards and wardens. Mandela had never taken dissent or criticism well. He was the son of a chief and the great-grandson of a king. He had to make some accommodations with the young men coming to Robben Island, though. Eventually the older and younger men found much to share with each other.

Bad news came in 1979. Winnie Mandela had survived her ordeal of solitary confinement a full decade ago, but she was now banned from Johannesburg and the townships, and she moved to Brandfort, 600 miles away. This did not make her trips to Robben Island any harder, but she was completely cut off from the support of her local community. Mandela anguished over what was happening to Winnie, but he could make no headway in appeals on her behalf.

Mandela's Family

Later in life, Mandela expressed considerable regret over what happened to his family members while he was in prison. Naturally, he had no control over these events, but he felt deep pain over them, nonetheless.

Thembi, Mandela's oldest son by Evelyn, died in a car accident in 1969. Mandela's mother died at around the same time. His daughters by his marriage to Winnie suffered terrible anxiety because they never knew when they might be separated from their mother. Winnie suffered the most of all.

Taken away in 1969, she was subjected to more than 100 days of solitary confinement. Hardened prisoners often relate being broken by just a few days in solitary, which they see as the most demeaning and painful punishment they can receive. Winnie bore up under this and survived the ordeal, but she spent more than a year in custody. Then, in 1979, she was taken away again and lived in exile at Brandfort, 600 miles from home. Only a very strong person could endure such isolation and suffering. Mandela admired his wife more and more as the years passed.

Such pain and loss can leave a deep wound, however. Winnie was never quite the same again after her period of solitary confinement. Though she was revered as "Mother of the Nation" by millions of blacks, she had lost touch with a core part of her soul, and that wound would re-emerge in the early 1990s.

Everything seemed to get even darker at the start of the new decade. In 1980, an international crisis in Iran and Afghanistan pitted the capitalist United States against the Communist Soviet Union. Americans voted in a new president that fall; Ronald Reagan intended to fight the Soviets to the finish, whether in military conflict or by economic means. The result was that the new Reagan administration smiled on the white South African government, which it saw as a steadfast ally in the fight against international communism. President Reagan never invited the South African president to the White House, but he spoke of constructive engagement with South Africa, hoping this would lead to an improvement in racial relations there.

Just when everything seemed at the lowest point, Mandela was told to pack his bags. He was leaving the island where he had spent the past 18 years.

CHAPTER 7

First Light

There were no preliminaries. Mandela was simply told to be ready to leave. There was no time for extended leave-taking with his comrades. He was shipped off the island that same day and moved to Pollsmoor Prison, on the mainland. This was only 12 miles from Robben Island, but it was a different world. There was no limestone to hack; no blinding sunlight with which to contend. Mandela lived in relative comfort. At first, he was with six other political prisoners, then on his own. There was time, now, to attend to the health concerns that had grown during his 18 years on Robben Island.

The white South African government had clearly decided to take no chances. Mandela must not die from neglect or disease; the international community was already coming down hard on South Africa. The visibility of black South Africans increased when Archbishop Desmond Tutu won the Nobel Peace Prize in the autumn of 1984.

Mandela knew more than he had in previous years. He was given plenty of newspapers to read and was more up to date on

Desmond Tutu

Many people think of Desmond Tutu when they think of Nelson Mandela, perhaps because the two men were the most visible leaders of the antiapartheid movement.

Born in Klerksdorp in 1931, Tutu was the son of a school-teacher and a washerwoman. He also went into teaching but left the profession because of the Bantu Education Act (1953), which prohibited blacks from studying advanced academic subjects. Tutu became first a priest, then a bishop in the Angli-can Church.

Tutu was a dozen years younger than Mandela. The differ-ence in their age and circumstances meant that Tutu did not become a leader for social justice until the early 1970s. He spent a number of years in Great Britain and the mountain kingdom of Lesotho, in Africa. After the Soweto riots of 1976 and the 1977 murder of Steve Biko, however, Tutu became the foremost champion of black freedom. Steve Biko was a South African political leader whose brutal beating and death while in police custody stunned and shocked people both within South Africa and elsewhere.

Tuto teased and taunted the white minority government of South Africa to a point where his life was in danger, but by winning the Nobel Peace Prize in 1984 he assured his physical safety. Made bishop of Johannesburg and then archbishop of Cape Town, Tutu was always at the forefront of conflict. Several times in the 1980s, he plunged into crowds that were intent on murdering people they thought were police informants. Tutu res-cued these men despite the danger to himself.

Tutu met with South African President P.W. Botha several times in the 1980s but made no headway in his effort to get the political prisoners released. In the end, it was international pressure that led to the release of Mandela, Walter Sisulu, and others. Archbishop Tutu remained a powerful presence in the new South Africa. At Mandela's request, he chaired the Truth and Reconciliation Commission that heard testimony between 1996 and 1998.

events than he had been in some time. Some of the news he received was pleasing and led to optimism, but other news must have left him discouraged. President Ronald Reagan continued to favor constructive engagement with the white South African government. Worse, violence was increasing throughout the land.

The year 1985 was the year the "necklace" was first employed and described. On a number of occasions, crowds of furious blacks turned on someone they believed to be a police informant, put a tire around his neck, doused it with gasoline, and set him afire. These "necklace" killings did much to harm the black cause, but there was little Mandela could do about it. He was dismayed to hear that his wife, Winnie, had been quoted as saying that the necklace killings were an appropriate response.

At Pollsmoor Prison, Winnie was now able to visit Mandela, and, for the first time in 18 years, they were able to touch. Meeting for the first kiss in nearly two decades was a memorable event. The passion between them was as strong as ever; perhaps it had even increased through the long absence, but the two made a commitment not to take their newfound freedom to its fullest expression, since this would be unfair to other political prisoners who had not received the freedoms Mandela enjoyed. Years later, Mandela was asked about this, whether it was hard not to enjoy what was possible. He responded:

> Well, it is easy. I mean, it's sometimes very difficult. I had to forget about things that you were used to. But, prison life, fortunately, I spent a lot of years, about 18 years with other prisoners and, as I say, they enriched your soul. The type of conversations we had, the experiences we shared.[23]

In 1985, President P.W. Botha made a surprising speech, claiming he would free Mandela if he would renounce violence in all cases whatsoever. Mandela had no way to express his answer; so he wrote a speech and gave it to his daughter Zindzi,

In 1985, South African President P.W. Botha, pictured here, promised Mandela freedom if he renounced violence for any cause. Mandela refused to give up his convictions in response to an ultimatum but later decided to initiate negotiations with the white South African government.

who read it aloud to a large Soweto crowd. Mandela would seek only an unconditional release:

> I cherish my own freedom dearly, but I care even more for your freedom. Too many have suffered for the love of freedom. I owe it to the widows, to their orphans, to their mothers and to their fathers who have grieved and wept for them. Not only I have suffered during these long, lonely wasted

years. I am not less life-loving than you are. But I cannot sell my birthright, nor am I prepared to sell the birthright of the people to be free.[24]

In that same year, Mandela made a decision on his own. He knew that most of his fellow prisoners were against having any talks with the white South African government, but Mandela believed the time had come. He was nearing 70, and if action did not come soon, it would be too late for him:

> There are times when a leader must move out ahead of his flock, go off in a new direction, confident he is leading his people the right way. Finally, my isolation furnished my orga-nization with an excuse in case matters went awry; the old man was alone and completely cut off, and his actions were taken by him as an individual, not a representative of the ANC.[25]

Talks began. They were quiet at first, with just Mandela and a few government officials. In every discussion, the South African government tried to create conditions for Mandela's release. He must renounce violence; he must persuade other ANC leaders to do the same; he must denounce communism. Mandela stayed with the conversations, but made no summary agreements. To him, it seemed a victory that the government was talking at all; he remembered many times, many years, when this had not been the case.

In the spring of 1988, a movement began in Britain called "Freedom at 70." Led by Father Trevor Huddleston—an Anglican priest who had spent many years in South Africa—the protest movement called for Mandela's freedom before his seventieth birthday, in July 1988. A huge rock concert was held at Wembley Stadium outside London, and millions of people watched the event on television. When the summer ended and Mandela was still a prisoner, though, some people began to lose hope.

At about this time, Mandela was transferred yet again. His new prison was called Victor Verster Prison, but it was truly like a gilded cage. Mandela lived in his own house, with his own cook and housecleaner. He could walk the grounds, even have an occasional friend over for dinner. This was like palace life after what he had endured on Robben Island, but, sad to say, there were some things that could not be made up. Try as he might, Mandela could not disguise his rapid aging at this point; he was no longer the vigorous man of the 1960s. The hard labor of two decades had taken something out of him.

His humor remained, however. On one occasion, a high South African official visited and found Mandela about to enjoy a breakfast of bacon and eggs. The official moved as if to take the tray, saying that Mandela's high blood pressure was a cause for concern. Mandela gripped the tray tightly and replied: "Major, I am sorry. If this breakfast will kill me, then today I am prepared to die."[26]

Visitors commented that Mandela, rather than being the prisoner, often seemed like the one in control. Something had enlarged his soul over the years, while simultaneously damaging his body. Helen Suzman visited him at Victor Verster Prison and remarked that he seemed like a king or prime minister.

For years, Mandela had asked for a meeting with South African prime minister and later president P.W. Botha. A formal meeting would give legitimacy to the African National Congress and, Mandela thought, make the bargaining process easier. For years, all his requests were denied, but in the summer of 1989, during Botha's presidency, Mandela was told he would meet him that very day.

Mandela was quite tense that morning. Botha was called the Great Crocodile by his staff; he had a formidable temper and often wagged his finger in an aggressive manner, to silence opposition. Mandela steeled himself to meet such patronizing behavior, but it turned out quite differently than he expected.

Mandela related their exchange: "He had his hand out and was smiling broadly, and in fact from that very first moment he completely disarmed me. He was unfailingly courteous, deferential, and friendly."[27]

The Mandela United Football Club

Winnie Mandela went through many changes in her life. Few were more surprising than her turn toward violence in the late 1980s. Vicious and criminal episodes that came to light in the late 1980s implicated Winnie and her "football club" in the kidnapping, torture, and even murder of police informants. Some have argued that she had been so brutalized during her period of solitary confinement, that she could not be held responsible for her actions. Others disagreed.

In 1985 or 1986, a group of local young toughs—some called them gang members—gathered around Winnie at her Orlando home, ostensibly to protect her. They called themselves the Mandela United Football Club and wore tracksuits that identified them as such in the neighborhood. This innocent-sounding name did not describe their actions, however. The young men rounded up and beat informants thought to be working with the police, subjecting them to torture and even death.

The most notorious example was the death of a 14-year-old boy, "Stompie" Seipei, reportedly at the hands of the football club. Winnie was tried and convicted for the crime, but given a suspended sentence. Later, during the Truth and Reconciliation Commission hearings, Archbishop Tutu implored Winnie to tell the whole truth about what had happened, but she refused. Winnie claimed to regret the actions of her football club but never took direct responsibility or apologized for her own or the club's actions. This drove a wedge between Nelson and Winnie, and after this time they were estranged.

There was no tension until Mandela asked the president to release all political prisoners, including himself, without delay. Botha firmly refused. Even so, the meeting was judged a success by all who were there. For the first time in more than a generation, a major white South African leader had sat down with a leader of the ANC. It is entirely possible that Mandela would have spent the rest of his life in prison, however, if not for the surprising events of the autumn of 1989.

Ever since 1961, Germany had been divided into East Germany, controlled by the Soviet Union, and West Germany, a capitalistic, democratic society. The demarcation had been the infamous Berlin Wall, built to prevent people leaving East Germany and moving to the West. In October 1989, though, millions of students and young people thronged the streets, and the Berlin Wall crumbled, both literally and figuratively. By early November, pieces of the Wall were being taken away as souvenirs, and the peoples of East and West Germany were physically reunited. (Their political reunification had to wait until 1991.) Other Eastern European nations followed suit, and by Christmas 1989, most of the Communist or Socialist governments of Europe had fallen like dominoes, replaced by new, popular governments.

South Africa was thousands of miles away, but the white government felt the repercussions. For the past generation, Pretoria had been able to count on Washington, D.C., for political support, because South Africa was a valuable Cold War ally. With Eastern European communism dead and the Soviet Union shown to be a paper tiger, the United States no longer needed to cozy up to the white minority government.

P.W. Botha resigned as president of South Africa in the fall of 1989. His successor, F.W. de Klerk, was as much of a hardliner as Botha, but he was also more realistic. South Africa could not afford further isolation in the international community and it could not afford economic sanctions. The new president began to meet with Mandela face to face. Around this time, a number

Mandela and his wife, Winnie, walked from Victor Vester Prison in February 1990. The world watched, stunned, as the frail old man emerged from prison. Coupled with the recent fall of the Berlin wall, Mandela's freedom signaled that a new age was at hand.

of political prisoners were released from Robben Island. Mandela showed no sadness that his time had not yet come; he was elated for the freedom of Walter Sisulu and others.

By this time, Mandela had been in Victor Verster Prison for seven years. He was as comfortable there as one could be in jail, and he believed he could bargain for good terms. Showing no anxiety to leave, Mandela bargained the white government down until there was nothing left to do but release the prisoner. In a stunning television address on February 2, 1990, F.W. de Klerk announced the imminent release of Nelson Mandela. The bans on both the African National Congress and the Pan-Africanist Congress were lifted: They became legal entities after nearly 30 years. Mandela walked out of Victor Verster on February 11, 1990.

The moment was unforgettable. Mandela came out, a little dazed by the sunshine and by the presence of television cameras. Technology had changed a good deal in the 27 years he had been locked away. Winnie joined her husband, and the two made a triumphant walk through part of Cape Town. They spent that night at Bishopscourt, the residence of Archbishop Desmond Tutu. The next day Mandela met the press and told the world the following:

> Today, the majority of South Africans, black and white, recognize that apartheid has no future. It has to be ended by our own decisive mass action in order to build peace and security. The mass campaign of defiance and other actions of our organizations and people can only culminate in the establishment of democracy.[28]

Mandela concluded by quoting himself, from the trial of 1964:

> I have fought against white domination and I have fought against black domination. I have cherished the ideal of a democratic and free society in which all persons live together

in harmony and with equal opportunity. It is an ideal which
I hope to live for and to achieve. But if needs be, it is an ideal
for which I am prepared to die.[29]

Luckily, he could now live. The pain of fighting for freedon was
over. Now it was on to the hard work of creating a new government and society.

CHAPTER 8

A New World

Millions of people around the world thrilled to the news of Mandela's release. A new decade had just started, and it seemed a new age had begun. Communist governments had fallen, Mandela was free, and apartheid would likely fall of its own weight. Mandela was careful not to be too optimistic. He loved the attention his new-found celebrity brought him, but, unlike many who received such accolades, he was not fooled by them.

A few days after his release, Mandela was back at 8115 Orlando East. His original home had burned in a fire in the 1980s, but it had been rebuilt. He and Winnie set up housekeeping, though they knew he would have very little time to spend there. There was not enough time to catch up with his large family. Through his two marriages, Mandela had 5 children and nearly 25 grandchildren (there were three great-grandchildren, too). He had always loved children and wanted to spend time with his own, but it could not be. The nation called him.

After a fast tour of parts of Western Europe and the United States, where he received a hero's welcome, Mandela came back to organize the African National Congress and begin negotiations with the white government under F.W. de Klerk. There were thorny obstacles, right from the start. De Klerk turned out to be a more formidable competitor than Mandela had thought he would be. A careful and clever politician, de Klerk seldom confronted Mandela but rather worked behind his back. The most dangerous issue had to do with the Zulu tribe and its cultural organization, called Inkatha.

The Zulus were the most militant of all the South African tribes; they had fought the British with great ferocity during the Zulu War of 1878 to 1879. They retained this warlike attitude a hundred years later, and in 1990 and 1991, Inkatha warriors made a number of shocking attacks on African National Congress groups. Even more disturbing, the Inkatha men were often escorted or helped by the South African white government. Mandela made a major speech in which he warned of a "Third Force" that disturbed the prospects for peace throughout South Africa. He chose not to identify Inkatha by name, but in private there were furious accusations and denials on all three sides: the African National Congress, the white South African government, and Inkatha.

F.W. De Klerk skillfully played Mandela and Mangosuthu Buthelezi, the leader of Inkatha, off one another. Both men suspected this duplicity, and there were bad feelings all around. Those between Mandela and de Klerk came to a head in May 1992, at a meeting of the Convention for a Democratic South Africa. De Klerk asked to speak last that day, and he used his opportunity to take broad swipes at the African National Congress, asking whether its members could ever be trusted to keep agreements once they were made. Even though the meeting was supposed to adjourn, Mandela rose, took the podium, and delivered a furious response:

> I am gravely concerned about the behavior of Mr. de Klerk today. He has launched an attack on the ANC and in doing so

Mangosuthu Buthelezi

Inkatha Freedom Party leader Mangosuthu Buthelezi is shown here in traditional tribal dress. Though Mandela wished to have a united South Africa, he and Buthelezi often butted heads regarding the political welfare of the country's citizens.

Born in 1928, Buthelezi had many things in common with Nelson Mandela. Both men were tribal chiefs and both were the descendants of kings. Buthelezi was a great-grandson of the Zulu king Cetewayo, who defied the British in the Zulu War of the late 1870s. Buthelezi and Mandela had both studied at the University College of Fort Hare, and both were progressive, forward-thinking tribal leaders. Their differences became apparent over time, however.

Buthelezi was committed to the advancement of the Zulu Nation within the greater South African one, and he was ready to make compromises that would lead to that end. Unlike Mandela, who wanted a truly unified South Africa, Buthelezi stayed close to his tribal roots and looked out for the Zulus before all others.

Buthelezi had repeatedly called for Mandela's release, but once that came about, the two men had a hard time finding common ground. Their animosity was never personal—they shared too many of the same values—but there was a great deal of fighting, both in word and with weapons, between the Inkatha and the African National Congress. Upon becoming president in 1994, Mandela made Buthelezi a key player in his administration, but their relations did not ease.

he has been less than frank. Even the head of an illegitimate, discredited minority government regime, as his is, has certain moral standards to uphold. He has no excuse just because he is the head of such a discredited regime not to uphold moral standards. . . . If such a man can come to a conference of this nature and play the type of politics he has played—very few people would like to deal with such a man.[29]

Though he concluded with some conciliatory gestures, these were some of the harshest words Mandela had ever used in public. Generally, he preferred a soft approach, but when truly provoked, he would raise up the lion within and demolish his opponents verbally, much as he had done in the philosophical discussions on Robben Island. F.W. de Klerk showed little emotion. He was a master politician; so was Mandela; and the two had met their match in one another.

Mandela never doubted that the negotiations had to continue. Even if he disliked and distrusted de Klerk, he had come too far— so had the nation—to back away now. So the talks continued. One of the thorniest questions had to do with amnesty or punishment. Hundreds, if not thousands, of crimes against humanity had been committed in the name of apartheid, and black South Africans wanted revenge. White South Africans could go along with negotiations, and perhaps even stomach a new government, but they would go down fighting rather than surrender many in their midst to the type of war crime tribunals that had taken place at the end of World War II.

Mandela and other members of the ANC were split on the matter. Many felt the nation could never truly be cleansed until people had been brought to justice, whereas others argued that the nation could never survive the bloodbath that would follow. In a sense, the stubbornness of F.W. de Klerk and other Afrikaners made Mandela's choice easier, since it was apparent there would be no agreement without a decision for amnesty. In the end, it was decided that a commission would be created to examine all the crimes against humanity that had taken place, and that those people who fully confessed to their crimes would be given amnesty.

As the agreements were being reached, Mandela took a few steps to make his home life more bearable. In 1991, his wife, Winnie, was accused and tried for the death of a 14-year-old boy named "Stompie" Seipei. He had been killed by members of Winnie's Mandela United Football Club because they thought he was a police informer, but it appeared she had been present and had done nothing to prevent the killing. She was found guilty and sentenced to six years in prison, but was given a suspended sentence. In 1992, Mandela and Winnie agreed to a formal separation. He made a rare display of public emotion, asking those present to understand all he had gone through. He professed a great and continuing love for Winnie but declared it would be better for all if they separated. In 1993, Mandela moved into a new home. He had come full circle, returning to the Transkei:

> I have always believed that a man should have a home within sight of the house where he was born. After being released from prison, I set about plans to build a country house for myself in Qunu. By the fall of 1993, the house was complete. It was based on the floor plan of the house I lived in at Victor Verster. People often commented on this, but the answer was simple: The Victor Verster house was the first spacious and comfortable home I ever stayed in, and I liked it very much. I was familiar with its dimensions, so at Qunu I would not have to wander in the night looking for the kitchen.[31]

Mandela did not tell the full truth. Living in Johannesburg had been a disappointment. Not only had his marriage broken up, but he was sometimes disappointed with the attitudes of his grandchildren. They came around every now and then, but not enough to warm the heart of a lonely old man.

WINNING THE NOBEL PEACE PRIZE

That old man was now 74, and he was running in his first nation-
wide election. Americans were impressed that Ronald Reagan
won the presidency when he was 69, but Reagan had spent decades
in the spotlight and was well versed in the mediums of radio and
television. Mandela had to overcome the perception that he was a
sort of Rip van Winkle; he had been gone from the world in the
years in which television had come to South Africa.

Mandela stood for the African National Congress and de
Klerk ran for the National Party. The two were opponents but
also comrades in arms, for they were joint recipients of the Nobel
Peace Prize for 1993. Mandela gave his acceptance speech on
December 10 (International Freedom Day) in Oslo, Norway:

> I would like to take this opportunity to congratulate my com-
> patriot and fellow laureate, State President F.W. de Klerk, on
> his receipt of this high honor.
>
> Together, we join two distinguished South Africans, the
> late Chief Albert Luthuli and His Grace Archbishop Desmond
> Tutu, to whose seminal contributions to the peaceful struggle
> against the evil system of apartheid you paid well-deserved
> tribute by awarding them the Nobel Peace Prize.[32]

Mandela looked forward to the end of the process of forming a
new government:

> At the southern tip of the continent of Africa, a rich reward is
> in the making, an invaluable gift in the preparation, for those
> who suffered in the name of all humanity when they sacrificed
> everything—for liberty, peace, human dignity and human
> fulfillment.[33]

The country boy from the Transkei spoke to the impressive crowd
in Norway, seeming to put together aspects from his long and rich
life experience:

Mandela is pictured with South African President F.W. de Klerk. The two man shared the Nobel Peace Prize on December 10, 1993. This was one of several times in Nobel Prize history that two or more men shared the honor. Ironically, the two men were also running against each other in the South African presidential election, to be held in April 1994.

> The children must, at last, play in the open veld, no longer tortured by the pangs of hunger or ravaged by disease or threatened with the scourge of ignorance, molestation and abuse, and no longer required to engage in deeds whose gravity exceeds the demands of their tender years.[34]

Mandela went on to pay tribute to Martin Luther King Jr., dead and gone these past 25 years:

> Let the strivings of us all prove Martin Luther King, Jr., to have been correct when he said that humanity can no longer

be tragically bound to the starless midnight of racism and war. Let the efforts of us all prove that he was not a mere dreamer when he spoke of the beauty of genuine brotherhood and peace being more precious than diamonds or silver or gold. Let a new age dawn![35]

Everyone there understood the irony. Mandela and de Klerk gratefully accepted the award, although they ran against each other in the first truly free election of their nation's history.

THE ELECTION

Mandela traveled incessantly. He was a master at handling crowds by now. He could take tea with Prime Minister Margaret Thatcher, speak to an Afrikaner about his farm, and do a quick dance at a local African village. Mandela was the supreme politician in the 1990s, rivaled only by U.S. President Bill Clinton, with whom he had a warm friendship.

There was little question that the African National Congress would win the election, but there were fears the process would be deemed illegitimate. Zulu Chief Buthelezi had the power to disrupt the whole matter; he urged his tribesmen not to vote in the April 1994 elections. There was sporadic violence in the weeks leading up to the election and genuine fears that the whole thing might be thrown off. At the last minute, however, Chief Buthelezi withdrew his objections. The Zulu did not vote in very high numbers, but enough of them came to the polls to make the process viable.

Mandela being Mandela, he joked about things. As he went to his polling station, he was asked for whom he would vote. Summoning up his most bemused expression, he said that he'd been thinking about that all day and still hadn't decided. This was vintage Mandela, the smooth statesman who never seemed to take himself too seriously.

South Africans turned out in great numbers, and the ballots took days to count. Soon, Mandela learned that he had been elected president and the ANC had won the overall election, with a bit less than the two-thirds majority for which they had hoped. That seemed fine with him; he did not want to seem to have a mandate for overhauling everything. Mandela's autobiography, *Long Walk to Freedom*, ends with his election and installation as new president of South Africa:

> I have walked that long road to freedom. I have tried not to falter. I have made missteps along the way. But I have discovered the secret that after climbing a great hill, one only finds that there are many more hills to climb. I have taken a moment here to rest, to steal a view of the glorious vista that surrounds me, to look back on the distance I have come. But I can rest only for a moment, for with freedom comes responsibilities, and I dare not linger, for my long walk is not yet ended.[36]

Chief of
the Nation

Mandela was the great-grandson of a king. His father had been the law in the little village of Qunu. Throughout a life full of uncertainty and setbacks, Mandela had maintained a chief-like attitude. Helen Suzman, after visiting him in jail, thought he acted more like a prime minister than a prisoner. Now he was chief of the nation, leader of all South Africa.

Mandela was inaugurated on May 10, 1994. His daughter, Zindi, sat beside him, and Archbishop Desmond Tutu offered the opening prayer. Winnie Mandela was there, conspicuously dressed, but she was kept well away from the podium. Mandela moved into the governor's palace in Cape Town. He could hardly believe the luxury that his office allowed him, but there was no relaxation in his work habits. He appeared tireless and was strictly punctual. He rarely took any liquor, preferring to sip a bit while others indulged. He even made time for exercise, his lifelong habit.

Many ANC members thought Mandela should hire an entirely new presidential staff, but he disagreed. He had always been intrigued by the challenge of meeting his former tormentors, and he

Archibishop Desmond Tutu congratulates newly elected South African President Nelson Mandela after his inauguration in May 1994. Tutu, a great friend of Mandela's, read the opening prayer of the ceremony and swore in the new president.

now seemed to delight in proving himself graceful in their midst. His Afrikaner bodyguards soon developed a powerful sense of loyalty to him; and his Afrikaner servants marveled at how he remembered their names and asked after their family members.

White South Africans were slowly won over by Mandela's charm and grace. He made a very public visit to the 94-year-old widow of former Prime Minister Verwoerd, the architect of apartheid, and stood for some time at the man's grave. The photograph of Mandela hugging the frail but still vibrant widow was amazing to the world. He also invited Percy Yutar, the lawyer who had prosecuted him and others in 1964. Yutar came for tea and went away saying Mandela was a living saint.

On a broader level, Mandela won over thousands, perhaps even millions, of Afrikaners through one symbolic gesture.

Afrikaners loved rugby, and many black South Africans had a negative view of the sport because during the days of apartheid, expressions that linked rugby to police brutality had abounded. So it was a tremendous surprise when President Mandela came on the field to present the winning trophy to the captain of the Springbok team in June 1995. Millions of people were watching the match on television, and most of them came away with a new appreciation for Mandela. In personal style, Mandela was a success from the very start. But he still had to contend with many political issues.

MANDELA'S CABINET

Mandela always sought consensus. His role model remained his adopted father, Jongintaba, regent of the Thembu tribe, who had listened to all opinions and come to his decisions slowly. Mandela made a point of having a variety of views in his cabinet. F.W. de Klerk was the second deputy president; Chief Betheluzi was minister of the interior; and there were many Afrikaners in the group.

There were many decisions to be made. South Africa, which had prospered in the 1960s and 1970s, had languished over the past decade. International sanctions had been useful for the anti-apartheid movement, but they also harmed the economy. Mandela had never been a Communist, but neither was he a rabid capitalist. Some in his party ranks hoped he would move South Africa in a socialist direction, but he did not. Mandela did his best to spur foreign investment: He wanted the economy to grow.

Mandela was often surprised by the growth of poverty during his years in prison. His home village of Qunu, for example, was poorer than when he was a boy, and there was polluted water, something he had never known in childhood.

The gold and diamond mines around Johannesburg still yielded much of the world's production of these precious metals, but they brought less profit than in the past. South Africa clearly

Mandela presents the Rugby World Cup trophy to South African team captain Francois Pienaar after the country defeated New Zealand in June 1995. For years, many black South Africans had a negative view of rugby, linking it to the harsh practices of the apartheid police, but Mandela's simple gesture reminded the world of his desire for unity.

needed to diversify its economy, so it could profit from a mix of agriculture and industry. Mandela was not skilled in economics, but he surrounded himself with people who were. South Africa did not make a quick pull out of the depression of the past decade, but progress was made. Then there was the matter of AIDS.

AIDS—ACQUIRED IMMUNODEFICIENCY SYNDROME

Mandela had been in prison during the years in which major public health improvements had been made. Tuberculosis was under control; polio had nearly disappeared. In 1982, however, about the time Mandela was transferred from Robben Island to Pollsmoor Prison, AIDS hit the international scene.

Acquired immunodeficiency syndrome (AIDS) does not kill outright. Instead, it weakens the immune systems of those it attacks, leaving them vulnerable to a host of illnesses, such as pneumonia. AIDS first appeared in the United States and in western European nations around 1982 and spread rapidly, but those nations had public health departments and public education with which to combat the spread of the disease. By the early 1990s, AIDS began to flourish in South Africa, a country with much fewer resources to marshall against it.

AIDS had existed in Africa to a limited extent, but it spread very rapidly in the 1990s. Many black South Africans had more than one wife—Mandela's father had four—and AIDS was most easily transmitted through sexual contact. The disease spread rapidly, and it was estimated that at least 5 million South Africans were infected with the virus by the year 2000.

Mandela knew nothing about AIDS until he came out of prison, and he was also quite ignorant about homosexual activity, which had contributed to the early spread of the disease in the United States and Western Europe. When he was first asked about the connection between homosexuality and AIDS, Mandela acted as if he did not believe there was such a thing as homosexuality, as if it were an aberrant behavior that disappeared when one was exposed to members of the opposite sex. He quickly learned from his mistake. It was clear that AIDS had become one of the greatest threats to the people of South Africa.

MANDELA, THE FOREIGN DIPLOMAT

Mandela was an expert in the art of personal diplomacy. Soon he was on a first-name basis with many leaders from around the world.

Critics of the Peacemaker

Mandela is surely one of the most admired and beloved men of modern times, but, like everyone else, he has his critics. Most of them begin by expressing their disagreements with his behavior toward the guards and wardens of Robben Island prison.

In the last six years of his prison sentence, Mandela received distinctly better treatment than the other political prisoners because the white South African government feared making a martyr of him. None of his fellow prisoners criticized him then, but his attitude upon release was hard for them to take. Mandela insisted on publicly forgiving most of the people who had incarcerated him; he had warm, heartfelt reconciliations with his former tormentors. No one doubted the sincerity of his feelings, for he had long since learned that forgiveness was one of the paths to mastery, but his fellow former inmates thought he was much too generous toward those who had done wrong.

Then, when he became president of South Africa in 1994, Mandela endured considerable criticism from within his own party ranks. Archbishop Desmond Tutu and Mandela had a public spat, in which the former accused Mandela's government of corruption. The two men publicly reconciled later that year, and Mandela made

He and Bill Clinton became close friends and political allies, and the same could be said for Mandela and Queen Elizabeth II. (The queen had long favored sanctions against the apartheid government, whereas U.K. Prime Minister Margaret Thatcher had not.)

Mandela also maintained friendships from earlier times. Despite the bad example shown by Muammar Qaddafi in the 1980s, Mandela remembered how Qaddafi and other Libyans had helped him in the days when he was a freedom fighter called the Black Pimpernel. He remained loyal to Qaddafi and also to Fidel Castro.

a point of naming Tutu as chairman of the Truth and Reconciliation Commission (TRC).

Still, there were other critics. In the late 1990s, Mandela's government appeared to be failing at attracting foreign investment and stabilizing the South African currency. He was assailed by the South African press and by foreign media, especially for his keeping the United States at arms length. In truth, this was not the case in the relationship between Mandela and Bill Clinton; they were always fast friends.

In what was one of his few public gaffes, Mandela stumbled in the winter of 2003. Noting that the United States was readying to attack Iraq, and that the U.N. Security Council had called for more time for sanctions to work, Mandela wondered aloud on TV whether this disrespect for the U.N. was because that organization was headed by a black man (Secretary General Kofi Annan). Mandela never apologized for this remark, which cost him the good will of quite a few people from foreign countries.

No man is an island. No man can live without others, and none can escape criticism. What can be said is that Mandela listened to critics, took what they said seriously, and sometimes—though not always—changed his stance.

Although he enjoyed excellent relations with Bill Clinton, Mandela was occasionally at odds with the American government. On one occasion, the United States threatened to apply pressure if South Africa sold weapons to Syria. Mandela retorted sharply that his government and country would find their own way, without the need to be told what to do.

Mandela was very conscious of the need to set a positive example for young African nations. Several, Niger and Rhodesia (now Zimbabwe) for example, had suffered badly when they changed from a white-run government to a black one. Economies had gone downhill; corruption had been widespread. There was absolutely no talk of personal corruption in Mandela's case: He seemed completely at ease with a low-cost lifestyle. There were levels of corruption within the government, however—some of them inherited from Afrikaner days and some of them only now coming to the surface.

Mandela knew how to apply the right type of pressure, but he could also be disarmingly helpful. Once a group of trade unionists camped outside the presidential palace, demanding to tell their grievances to the president. He slipped out another door and appeared among them quite suddenly. This did not mean he supported their aims, or agreed with their tactics; it meant he appreciated the need for every voice to be heard.

TRUTH AND RECONCILIATION COMMISSION

Mandela thought of himself as old; he turned 76 the year he became president. Some of those around him thought of him as younger, but he considered himself a man out of touch with modern-day issues. Economics interested him; AIDS befuddled him at first, and he was not always sure how to proceed in addressing it. In one key matter, however, he felt truly qualified to advance the cause of his people: the issues of truth and reconciliation.

Mandela had already shown himself supreme at the art of forgiveness. He could have been much more vengeful toward those

Looking out of the barred window of Mandela's former prison cell at Robben Island, U.S. President Bill Clinton listens as Mandela describes the unfavorable conditions he endured there. Mandela gave a tour of the facility, which is now a government-run tourist attraction, to Clinton and his family in 1998.

who had harmed him. As president, he could have turned the tables. He did not do so; instead, he urged forgiveness and reconciliation, but he stressed the importance of knowing the truth. South Africa could not overcome the legacy of apartheid so long as any part of it remained in the shadows. To bring everything to the light, Mandela formed the Truth and Reconciliation Commission (TRC). He asked Archbishop Desmond Tutu to head this important group.

The TRC met for the first time on December 17, 1995. This was the anniversary of the Afrikaner (Boer) victory over the

Xhosa tribes at the Battle of Blood River, and it had long been a national holiday. Now it was remade into Freedom Day. Desmond Tutu and 16 other members formed the TRC. They set an elaborate set of ground rules to govern the process, but even these were found to be inadequate. As time progressed, more and more perpetrators of hideous crimes came forward to testify, and TRC members were sometimes shocked and sickened to the core.

Mandela did not attend the hearings. He felt that as president, he was better off staying away from the details, leaving them, instead, in Desmond Tutu's hands. There was no denying the force of what came from the hearings, however. Apartheid had made humans into hideous caricatures of themselves. Afrikaner security police confessed to roasting men alive (apparently this took about seven hours). Inkatha warriors testified to receiving

Mandela and Celebrities

Mandela is one of the most photographed and admired men in the world, but he has never really gotten over his admiration for others. He delights in spending time with Michael Jackson, Whitney Houston, and many other pop stars. Like John F. Kennedy, Mandela has a natural feel for celebrities, and he seems more relaxed with them than with his own cabinet members.

Mandela has made friends with President Bill Clinton and many other leading people of the day. He has taken special pleasure in showing his friends Robben Island, which has been transformed into a national historic park. One of the most poignant photographs shows Mandela side by side with President Clinton, examining the little windows out of which he once gazed.

Mandela also travels to the United States on occasion. He had a memorable television interview with Larry King in the summer of 2000. King learned that Mandela and Winnie had not taken advantage of the private time they could have had together when the restrictions of Mandela's imprisonment were loosened during the 1980s. He pressed the point, asking if it was not very difficult for a loving man like Mandela to forego money from the white South African government so they could continue their "black-on-black" violence. Finally, and perhaps most disturbing of all, some African National Congress members confessed to crimes committed on behalf of the antiapartheid movement.

There was enough blame to go around. There was enough horror generated by the truth telling to demolish the fragile good will that had developed between the black and white communities in South Africa, but the TRC continued its work. Some of the most painful revelations had to do with Winnie, Mandela's former wife (the couple formally divorced in 1996).

Winnie testified to the TRC for a total of 9 days. She and the Mandela United Football Club were accused of a number of atrocities, including the killing of police informants. Archbishop

time with his wife. Mandela answered with great smoothness that no, it was very easy, because he and Winnie were part of a great struggle that was larger than themselves. It was easy to forego when they knew they did it as part of the cause. King was on to something. He saw that curious blend in Mandela's soul: the blend of the passionate freedom fighter with the abstemious saint.

King also asked how Mandela thought he should be regarded:

> KING: You had a remarkable life, what do you think about it? What do you want us to think about you?

> MANDELA: No, that must be left to future generations, because what happens today may not be shared by future generations. So, it's better for us to leave to others to charge the role which one has played.*

---

*Mandela, conversation with Larry King, quoted in "President Nelson Mandela One-on-One." *Larry King Live*. Aired May 16, 2000, 9:00 P.M. ET. Available at http://transcripts.cnn.com/TRANSCRIPTS/0005/16/lkl.00.html.

Desmond Tutu was inclined to go softly with Winnie. He pointed out that his family and hers lived on the same block, Orlando Street, and that she was the godmother of one of his grandchildren. Tutu implored, even begged, Winnie to tell the whole truth about what had happened and to show remorse. She did not do so. Perhaps she was too scarred by her time in solitary confinement in 1969 or her banishment to Brandfort (1979–1985), or perhaps the divorce had made her bitter. Whatever the reason, she was unrepentant. Mandela never commented on his former wife's testimony. He did his best to stay away from the whole matter, but it must have caused him great pain. Winnie was the love of his life, his great source of strength during the years he was in prison. How could things have gone so horribly wrong?

Desmond Tutu handed the final TRC report to Mandela at the end of October 1998. A great deal of work had gone into this project, which yielded five volumes of testimony and decision-making. Mandela accepted it gravely.

Mandela's term as president of South Africa was up in 1999. He did not run for another term; he was happy to see his friend Thabo Mbeki become the new president. Mandela's political career was over, but his personal life was about to flourish.

CHAPTER 10

Golden
Years

Mandela had to wait for personal happiness. He had to wait most of his life, in fact. This does not mean he failed to enjoy life. Far from it. He had always found pleasure, often in small things like the voices and sounds of children, or the thrill of eating bacon and eggs after having been denied such things for so long. For great and lasting happiness, though, he had to wait until he was 80 years old.

Her name was Graça; she was the widow of the former president of Mozambique, Samora Machel. She was quite young when Mandela went into prison, and he knew little of her in those years. When her husband was killed in an airplane accident in 1986, however, he sent her a letter from Pollsmoor Prison, and she responded in a way that tells us much in a few words: "From within your vast prison, you brought a ray of light in my hour of darkness."[37]

Born in 1945, Graça had been educated at the University of Lisbon. She helped in the freedom struggle against the Portuguese colonial powers in Mozambique and became the first female cabinet minister of her country in 1975. Soon after, she married

Mandela and his new wife, Graça Machel, share in a joint celebration of their wedding and Mandela's birthday in July 1998. Machel, widow of the former president of Mozambique, was a political activist in her own right. She helped rid Mozambique of Portuguese colonial rule and became the country's first female cabinet minister in 1975.

the country's new president. He already had six children, so she began married life with a large family.

Graça and Mandela continued to correspond after he was released from prison. It is not known where they first met, but members of Mandela's presidential household were the first to notice the frequent trips to Mozambique and the growing affection between the two. They had much to share. He had the wisdom acquired through a lifetime of service, struggle, and sacrifice; she had the youthful energy of a person who had many good years to come. Mandela was full of praise for her: "I'm in love with a remarkable lady. I don't regret the reverses and setbacks because late in life I am blossoming like a flower, because of the love and support she has given me. . . . She is the boss. When I am alone I am very weak."[38]

After his divorce from Winnie in 1996, Mandela was free to pursue the new love of his life. They were seen together more frequently throughout 1997 and the early part of 1998. Rumors abounded, but the couple denied they had any major plans. It was all an elaborate deception, for on July 17, 1998, one day before his eightieth birthday, Mandela married Graça in a private ceremony. The next day served as both his birthday and the formal celebration of the wedding. Pop stars abounded. Michael Jackson was there. This was the biggest birthday party of Mandela's long life, and, with the exception of some early childhood memories, the happiest.

Retirement suited Mandela perfectly. He doted on his grandchildren and on Graça's children by her marriage to Samora Machel. He kept mostly to his personal life; only occasionally did he speak out on international affairs.

SCANDALS AND WAR

One of Mandela's best friends from his days as president was U.S. President Bill Clinton. When Clinton fell into trouble with a scandal involving White House intern Monica Lewinsky,

Mandela addresses a joint sitting of Parliament in Cape Town in May 2004. Speaking against the war in Iraq, the South African president criticized both the U.S. and British governments in their defiance of the United Nations' requests for restraint.

Mandela was one of the loudest voices in Clinton's defense. One does not progress from glory to glory, he said, but shows one's greatness by rising time and time again from one's mistakes and errors. Coming from someone who had endured prison and infamy, yet had risen to the top, these were strong words indeed.

Mandela also spoke out against the 2003 U.S. military operations against Saddam Hussein's Iraq, allegedly because the Hussein regime harbored weapons of mass destruction. The United Nations tried to restrain America, but President George W. Bush pushed ahead with plans for war, just the same. Mandela appeared on television, asking the plaintive question: "Is it because the Secretary-General of the United Nations is now a black man? They never did that when Secretary-Generals were white."[39] Later, Mandela would make similar comments about other American intrusions into the Arab world. Was this because the people were black, brown, or otherwise colored?

These comments fell rather flat because President George W. Bush had geared the American people up for war with Iraq. When no weapons of mass destruction were found, however, some of Mandela's comments were accepted, albeit grudgingly.

MORE PERSONAL LOSSES

Old age has its compensations, but health often is not high on the list. As he lived into his eighties, Mandela found many former friends and colleagues gone. The losses mounted up.

Perhaps the most painful was the death of his oldest living son, Makgatho, in January 2005. Father and son had not been close for many years; it was not easy to see why. Soon after his son's death, though, Mandela revealed that Makgatho had died from AIDS, the virus that was sweeping through every level of South African society. As was his practice, Mandela used this loss as an opportunity to speak out on a major issue—to urge young people to be tested for the virus—but his pain was evident.

THE MAN AND THE LEGEND

By his eighty-fifth birthday in 2002, Mandela was a legend in his own time. Young people around the globe often recalled that seeing him released from prison in 1990 was their first introduction

The Peacemaker's Successor

Everyone knew it would be difficult to replace Mandela. There were those who thought he should remain in office until the end of his life, but Mandela believed he deserved some peaceful years in the time that remained for him. In 1997, he supported Thabo Mbeki's candidacy for president of the African National Congress, and in 1998, he endorsed Mbeki in the national presidential election. Mbeki took office in June 1999.

Born in 1942, Mbeki came from the Transkei, the same homeland as Mandela. Twenty-four years separated the two, so they did not know each other in the early years of struggle against apartheid, but Mbeki's father served prison time on Robben Island along with Mandela.

Like his father, Mbeki was a member of the South African Communist Party. After his father was arrested, Mbeki left South Africa and spent almost 30 years in political exile in England, Communist Russia, Zambia, Botswana, and elsewhere. As a result, Mbeki became acquainted with a wider pan-African struggle against colonialism as well as against apartheid.

Mbeki returned to South Africa in 1990, where he became one of Mandela's closest advisers. This does not mean they agreed on all subjects. Mandela had become a firm believer in nonviolence while Mbeki was more militant. In 1997, Mbeki was one of a group of African National Congress leaders who applied to the Truth and Reconciliation Commission for amnesty for unspecified violations of human rights. Critics of Mbeki point to this difference between him and Mandela; supporters point out that Mandela was in prison—and therefore removed from the violent struggle—during the 1960s, 1970s, and 1980s. Mbeki had this to say on the occasion of the new South African Constitution in 1996:

to international politics and world affairs. He guided South Africa through an extremely tense and critical time, and, if the results were not perfect, most people acknowledged things would have been worse if he were not at the helm. Reporters admitted to being

I am an African. I am born of the peoples of the continent of Africa. The pain of the violent conflict that the peoples of Liberia, Somalia, the Sudan, Burundi, and Algeria experience is a pain I also bear.*

Upon becoming South Africa's president, Mbeki announced he would continue in Mandela's path. By 1999, Mbeki had shed the communism of his early years; in fact, he became an ardent supporter of attracting more foreign investment into South Africa. The biggest problems the country faced were poverty and AIDS.

Poverty had always been a South African problem, but the new economy of the 1990s made things worse. Mbeki, Mandela, and others were shocked at how formerly dignified rural workers had become desperate people, some of them looking for government handouts. Mandela before, and Mbeki afterward, both rejected this notion. They wanted South Africa to be a land of proud, independent people.

AIDS was even more disastrous than poverty. In the years before AIDS appeared, many South Africans had believed that a man had the right to have sexual relations with as many people as he desired. This promiscuity led to South Africa having one of the highest rates of AIDS in the world.

By the early twenty-first century, Mbeki had done a good job of continuing the Mandela legacy. If he lacked Mandela's charisma, he had the steady head and cool resolve needed to lead this troubled nation into a new time.

---

*Terence Corrigna. *Mbeki: His Time Has Come*. South African Institute of Race Relations, 1999, p. 44.

As a congratulatory gesture, Mandela raises the hand of newly elected African National Congress President Thabo Mbeki during the ANC's fiftieth general congress in December 1997. Mandela was content to allow his friend to assume leadership of the country.

hopelessly charmed by Mandela. He was so attentive to them, so human and warm that it was almost impossible to maintain one's objectivity in his presence. Still, some people wondered: How much was the man and how much was the mask?

Those who knew him best asserted that the man and mask were one. Something had happened to Mandela in those 27 years of prison, something that lifted him to a higher plane of the universal human condition. It was not that he lacked faults, but rather that he stayed impeccable despite them. Try as they might, no reporter, journalist, or debunker was able to show that Mandela was corrupt, endorsed corruption, or slacked off when it came to his friends. He was a man relatively free from stain.

As we look at the close of the twentieth century, with the fall of the Soviet Union and the end of apartheid, we see that the 1990s were a decade of extraordinary change. Many people and situations have been given credit for the end of Russian Communism and the fall of the Berlin Wall, but to Nelson Mandela must go the largest share of credit for dismantling apartheid and creating a new South Africa, one of equality before the law and equality of opportunity. He was one of those rare individuals who had a dream and was lucky enough, fortunate enough, or privileged enough to see it come true.

1899–1902	Afrikaners fight the British in the Anglo–Boer War.
1910	The Union of South Africa is established.
1912	The African National Congress is established.
1914	World War I begins; many Afrikaners resist participation.
1918	Nelson Mandela is born in the Transkei region of South Africa.
Circa 1919	Mandela's father is deprived of his chieftain status.
1927	Mandela and his mother go to the Great Place.
1938	Mandela enters the University College of Fort Hare.
1939	World War II begins; Afrikaners vote to participate, but narrowly.
1941	Mandela and Justice run away from home to Johannesburg.
1944	Mandela marries Evelyn Mase.
1945	Their first son, Thembi, is born; Graça Simbine is born in Mozambique.
1946	Protest strikes and boycotts begin.
1948	The National (Afrikaner) Party wins the national election.
1952	Resistance movement begins as Afrikaners celebrate 300th anniversary of their arrival in South Africa; Mandela and Oliver Tambo open their legal practice.

1955	The Freedom Charter of the African National Congress is issued in Kliptown.
1956	Mandela and 127 others are arrested; the Freedom Trial begins.
1958	Mandela divorces Evelyn and marries Winnie.
1960	Mandela forms the Spear of the Nation section of the African National Congress.
1960	Mandela's first daughter with Winnie, Zindzi, is born.
1961–1962	Mandela goes abroad to seek training in guerrilla warfare.
1963	Mandela is arrested and sent to Robben Island.
1964	The Rivonia Trial ends in life imprisonment for Mandela; Mandela commences his sentence on Robben Island.
1966	Prime Minister Verwoerd is assassinated; prison conditions worsen.
1967	Chief Albert Luthuli dies in his Zulu homeland.
1969	Mandela's mother and his oldest son, Thembi, die in the same year; Winnie is taken into solitary confinement.
1976	The Soweto riots begin.
1982	Mandela is taken from Robben Island to Pollsmoor Prison, on the mainland; Mandela has his first face-to-face meeting with Winnie in 17 years.
1984	Desmond Tutu wins the Nobel Peace Prize.

1985 Black–white relations worsen with "necklace" killings of police informants.

1986 Mandela begins talking with white government officials.

1988 British sympathizers organize the "Freedom at 70" movement.

1989 Communist governments are toppled throughout Eastern Europe.

1990 Mandela is freed; he negotiates with the Afrikaner government.

1991 "Black-on-black" violence grows.

1992 Mandela and Winnie separate; violence, especially black against black, escalates.

1993 Agreement is reached for elections to be held in the coming year.

1994 Mandela is elected president of the new South Africa; he is sworn in at a ceremony at Cape Town.

1995 Mandela initiates the Truth and Reconciliation Commission.

1996 Mandela and Winnie divorce.

1997 Mandela becomes an international celebrity, with many other world leaders seeking his counsel and support.

1998 Desmond Tutu hands the five-volume TRC report to Mandela; Mandela celebrates his eightieth birthday and marries Graça Machel.

1999 Mandela leaves office.

2000   He is interviewed by Larry King in the United States.

2003   Mandela celebrates his eighty-fifth birthday.

2005   His oldest living son, Makgatho, dies of AIDS.

NOTES

Chapter 1
1. *Time* (June 19, 1964: p. 25).
2. Ibid.

Chapter 2
3. Nelson Mandela, *Long Walk to Freedom: The Autobiography of Nelson Mandela* (Boston: Little, Brown, 1994, p. 3).
4. Ibid., p. 13.
5. Ibid., p. 15.
6. Ibid., pp. 18–19.
7. Ibid., p. 19
8. Ibid., p. 45.

Chapter 3
9. Eve Palmer and Geoffrey Jenkins, *The Companion Guide to South Africa* (London: Collins, 1978, p. 15).
10. Mandela, *Long Walk to Freedom,* p. 83.

Chapter 4
11. Ibid., p. 144.
12. Ibid., p. 151.
13. John Vail, *Nelson and Winnie Mandela* (Philadelphia: Chelsea House, 1989, p. 51).

Chapter 5
14. Mandela, *Long Walk to Freedom,* p. 263.
15. Ibid., pp. 297–298.
16. Anthony Sampson, *Mandela: The Authorized Biography* (New York: Knopf, 1999, p. 195).

17. Ibid., p. 350.
18. Mandela, *Long Walk to Freedom,* p. 350.

Chapter 6
19. Ibid., p. 378.
20. Ibid., p. 388.
21. Ibid., p. 389.
22. Quoted in, Sampson, *Mandela: The Authorized Biography,* p. 231.

Chapter 7
23. Mandela, conversation with Larry King, quoted at "President Nelson Mandela One-on-One." *Larry King Live.* Aired May 16, 2000. Available at http://transcripts.cnn.com/ TRANSCRIPTS/0005/16/lkl.00. html.
24. Kader Asmal, David Chidester, and Wilmot James, eds., *Nelson Mandela, In His Own Words* (Boston: Little, Brown, 2003, pp. 46–47).
25. Mandela, *Long Walk to Freedom,* pp. 458–459.
26. Ibid., p. 472.
27. Ibid., p. 479.
28. Asmal, et al., *Nelson Mandela, In His Own Words,* p. 60.
29. Ibid., p. 62.

Chapter 8
30. Mandela, *Long Walk to Freedom,* p. 520.
31. Ibid., p. 529.

32. Asmal, et al., *Nelson Mandela, In His Own Words*, p. 507.
33. Ibid., p. 508.
34. Ibid., p. 508.
35. Ibid., p. 510.
36. Mandela, *Long Walk to Freedom*, p. 544.

Chapter 10
37. Sampson. *Mandela: The Authorized Biography*, p. 541.
38. Ibid., p. 549.
39. "Nelson Mandela." Wikipedia. Available at http://en.wikipedia.org/wiki/Nelson_Mandela.

BIBLIOGRAPHY

Cowell, Alan. *Why Are They Weeping? South Africans Under Apartheid.* New York: Stewart, Tabori & Chang, 1988.

Harrison, Nancy. *Winnie Mandela.* New York: George Braziller, 1986.

Mandela, Nelson. *Long Walk to Freedom: The Autobiography of Nelson Mandela.* Boston: Little, Brown, 1994.

Mandela, Nelson. *The Struggle Is My Life: His Speeches and Writings.* New York: Pathfinder, 1986.

Palmer, Eve, and Geoffrey Jenkins. *The Companion Guide to South Africa.* London: Collins, 1978.

Sampson, Anthony. *Mandela: The Authorized Biography.* New York: Knopf, 1999.

Suzman, Helen. *In No Uncertain Terms: A South African Memoir.* New York: Knopf, 1993.

Books

Mandela, Nelson. *Long Walk to Freedom: The Autobiography of Nelson Mandela*. Boston: Little, Brown, 1994.

Reader's Digest. *The Real Story: Illustrated History of South Africa*. Pleasantville, New York: Reader's Digest, 1988.

Vail, John. *Nelson and Winnie Mandela*. Philadelphia: Chelsea House, 1989.

Web sites

"Nelson Mandela," Wikipedia.
http://en.wikipedia.org/wiki/Nelson_Mandela

Mandela, conversation with Larry King, quoted at "President Nelson Mandela One-on-One." *Larry King Live*.
http://transcripts.cnn.com/TRANSCRIPTS/0005/16/lkl.00.html

PICTURE CREDITS

ABOUT THE AUTHOR

SAMUEL WILLARD CROMPTON is a historian and biographer who lives in the Berkshire Hills of western Massachusetts. Crompton has written many books for Chelsea House, including *Emanuel Swedenborg* and *Desmond Tutu*. He has a keen interest in biographies of spiritual leaders, and he attended the Spirituality in Education conference in Boulder, Colorado, in 1997.